MATH HACKS ²

STRESS LESS + DO BETTER

Vanessa "The Math Guru" Vakharia

Illustrations by Hyein Lee

D0989073

Scholastic Canada Ltd.
Toronto New York London Auckland Sydney
Mexico City New Delhi Hong Kong Buenos Aires

This book goes out to anyone who has ever faced a problem that feels impossible to figure out. This book is a reminder to YOU that the best part about solving a problem isn't the actual solution, but all of the cool stuff you learn about yourself in the process!

This book would not exist if it weren't for all of the very special humans who made it happen! Huge, huge thanks to: Ewa Kasinska, Erin O'Connor, Yvonne Lam, Erin Haggett, Hyein Lee, and Maral Maclagan. And of course, extra love to my parents, sister, and every student, parent, and tutor that has been part of The Math Guru community and who make my math-world spin round and round so magically!

— Vanessa Vakharia

Scholastic Canada Ltd.
604 King Street West, Toronto, Ontario M5V 1E1, Canada

Scholastic Inc.
557 Broadway, New York, NY 10012, USA

Scholastic Australia Pty Limited
PO Box 579, Gosford, NSW 2250, Australia

Scholastic New Zealand Limited
Private Bag 94407, Botany, Manukau 2163, New Zealand

Scholastic Children's Books
Euston House, 24 Eversholt Street, London NW1 1DB, UK

www.scholastic.ca

Library and Archives Canada Cataloguing in Publication

Title: Math hacks 2 : stress less + do better / Vanessa "The Math Guru" Vakharia ; illustrations by Hyein Lee.

Other titles: Math hacks two
Names: Vakharia, Vanessa, author. | Lee, Hyein, illustrator.
Identifiers: Canadiana 20210124334 | ISBN 9781443182843 (softcover)
Subjects: LCSH: Mathematics—Juvenile literature.
Classification: LCC QA40.5 .V34 2021 | DDC j510—dc23

Photos ©: cover background, 69 and throughout: Shutterstock.com;
4 left: Photo courtesy the author; 4 right: Ben Powless.

6 5 4 3 2 1   Printed in China 62   21 22 23 24 25

Table of Contents

YOU CAN BE A MATH SUPERSTAR!

So, who even am I and why did I write this?

Me then, before I knew I was a math SUPERSTAR.

Me now, rocking my math AND my music!

Oh hey there! If you read my first book, Math Hacks, you might already know me. And if you didn't, no sweat — it's nice to finally meet you! My first book had lots of good info about the basics of adding, subtracting, multiplying, dividing, decimals and fractions. But there is SO much other cool math stuff out there, so I decided to write this book that you're reading RIGHT now.

In case you don't already know this . . . I failed math in high school. TWICE!!! When I was younger, I didn't really love math so much. I didn't understand it, it stressed me out and it wasn't fun to do. But one day, a teacher explained math to me in a way I had never heard anyone explain it. It was like this bright light bulb went on in my head — POOF!

I suddenly realized: Hey, I'm not bad at math AT ALL, I just never heard it explained the right way for ME!

My whole life changed after that. I realized that math is actually SO cool once you get it — and ANYONE can do it. Even me. And that means you too! Once you figure out you can do math — even if you've spent your entire life thinking you can't — well, you'll realize you can do ANYTHING! Even things that seem hard or impossible. Now I'm a math teacher, a podcast host, an author and an entrepreneur. I started The Math Guru, the coolest tutoring studio ever (obviously!), where we teach math and science to kids in Toronto in person, and all around the world online. When I'm not rocking my math, I love being an actual rockstar, so I started my very own band called Goodnight, Sunrise. I have so much fun writing songs, playing keytar and jumping around on big stages wearing lots of glitter.

I wrote Math Hacks[2] to help you find YOUR inner math superstar. Because trust me, it's in there somewhere!

How should YOU use this book?

You can use this book whatever way feels best to you. The first part is all about YOU (yay!): how you can feel more chill with math and rock the time you put into your work. The second part is the ACTUAL math. Here are a few tips that might help you get the most out of it.

#1: Think of me as your BFF! But for real, when you're reading this book, picture ME (a happy, smiley, chill person) doing math with YOU, just like your best friend would!

#2: Follow your math-heart! If you need help with a specific math topic, just head on over to that section. You don't have to read this book in order or spend time reading stuff you already get! But sometimes it's good to read stuff you already understand — you might find a cool new way of looking at it.

#3: Don't give up! I obviously couldn't fit EVERY single math thing in here because the book would have been too big to carry. So I tried to cover the stuff that most kids have questions about. If you can't find what you're looking for, keep trying! Check out the first Math Hacks book, or talk to your teacher or caregiver for extra help.

#4: You do you! If you understand something a different way than I've explained it, that's totally okay — AWESOME even! Everyone learns differently and that's what makes us so cool. I've explained stuff in a way that I find most kids understand, but YOU pick the way YOU get it best.

#5: Play along We learn math best by doing practice problems. That's why we include questions that are fully worked out. Once you think you get it, write out the question on a separate sheet of paper and try to do the WHOLE thing yourself without looking at what's in the book. Then check to see if you got it right . . . and if not, retrace your steps to see where you went wrong, and try again!

PART 1

YOU HACK YOU!

CONFIDENCE HACKS

You are AWESOME — don't you forget it!

Feeling positive about math is only partly about the actual math. The other part has to do with feeling great . . . about YOURSELF! If you feel seriously good about yourself, you're more likely to keep trying when math problems get extra tricky or when ANYTHING gets tough. So we're going to build your CONFIDENCE muscles as well as your math ones! When you're feeling like maybe you just can't, these confidence hacks will help you know that you totally CAN.

#1: Remember when? Right now stuff you're learning may seem im-poss-i-ble, but guess what? I bet you that a LOT of the stuff you're good at now felt impossible once upon a time. You're just so good at those things now that you totally FORGET that they used to be hard. Don't believe me? Was it easy for you to learn how to tie your shoes at first? Or remember the difference between left and right? Or learn a new remote?

Nope! Those things were frustrating, but you're probably an expert at them now. So next time something seems impossible and you feel bummed out, remember that you have learned how to do SO many hard things already! Give yourself a high five and keep on trying. You'll get there eventually, SUPERSTAR!

#2: The awesome swap Sometimes when you're feeling down it's hard to think of just why we're SO AWESOME! My super-secret tip? Call your best friend and do an awesomeness-swap! What's that? You write a list of things that are awesome about your friend, and they write a list of awesome things about you — and you swap. Read the list of how you're awesome whenever you start feeling like you can't do anything.

BONUS: You might even find that helping another person feel awesome makes YOU feel pretty good too! When I'm feeling blue I remember to say something nice to someone else. Putting a smile on THEIR face usually puts one on mine. It can be easy things like "What a great colour on you" or "you have the BEST laugh" or "you like the coolest music." Now, go give it a try!

#3: Make a superstar spread It's a collage all about YOU — the things you love and that make you feel great. This could be pics of you playing your fave sports or with your friends, ribbons you earned, hilarious birthday cards, lyrics to your favourite song. Seriously, anything that lights you up inside. Write your name BIG and FANCY across the middle of an art board and decorate away. What else are you saving that glitter for? Hang it up where you can see it when you're doing homework. Next time you feel blech, really look at it to remind yourself of all the ways that you are AWESOME.

#4: Don't be mean to your BFF You would never be mean to your best friend, right? Best friends are nice and stand up for each other. So you need to start doing that for YOURSELF. If a negative voice pops into your head saying "you can't do this," answer back with a "Hey! Don't talk to my friend that way!" And just like you'd do something nice for a friend who's feeling a bit down, remember to treat your best friend (YOU, remember?!) to a nap, funny joke, or your favourite PJs if you've had a bad day. You'll find that negative voice in your head becoming a lot nicer.

#5: Make mistakes One of the best ways to build confidence is to make mistakes — lots of them! Seriously! Putting up your hand or taking a shot on goal seem like big chances to totally blow it. But you need to get to a point where those challenges feel fun instead of scary and the best way to do that is just to go for it. Give the wrong answer. Give another one. Miss that goal and three more after that. You'll find that it's not the huge, scary, big deal that you THOUGHT it was going to be. Who cares?! The more you get used to making mistakes, the more you realize that they aren't so bad after all. Trying new things can help us feel powerful. And they make life fun. So next time you're worried about sucking at something, GET OUT THERE and try it anyway.

#6: Mantra magic A mantra is a magical sentence or motto that you can use to make you feel like your best self! Some of my favourites are "I am a great problem solver!" and "I am the only me in the whole world!" and "I have AMAZING ideas!" Now it's your turn — invent your very own. And whenever you're feeling not-so-hot, repeat it five times in your head. Write it down. Say it out loud. Even yell it at the top of your lungs — whatever works for you to cheer yourself on.

#7: You do YOU Sometimes it's easy to feel like we're not good enough, smart enough, fast enough or whatever enough. It's so easy to constantly compare ourselves to someone else. Newsflash: you will never be someone else and you shouldn't want to be! The coolest part about you is that you are YOU and no one else will ever be as good at that as you are! HOW COOL IS THAT? It's okay to have role models, and to work on getting better at stuff — that's all a part of learning and growing up. But don't ever compare yourself to them because you're totally different people. Always remember to compare yourself to who you were yesterday, NOT to who someone else is today. That's where the magic is!

#8: Choose again Sometimes mean thoughts creep into our heads that make us feel bad about ourselves. For example, you might be writing a math test and hear a voice in your head that says "You suck at math!" or "You can't do this!" When this happens to me, I choose again. That means that when a negative thought pops in my head, I simply choose a BETTER, more positive thought. So, instead of "You suck at math!" I choose a thought like "There's a lot of math you're good at, some is just tricky sometimes!" And instead of "You can't do this!" I flip it to "Trying is half the battle — just go for it!" It's kind of like a choose-your-own-adventure story except you pick your own attitude. Now YOU give it a try!

CHILL-OUT HACKS
Relax! It's only math.

A few years ago, I was a contestant on the TV game show Canada's Smartest Person. One of the show's challenges was about MATH! We all had to pretend we were cashiers at a grocery store and calculate change. The host asked, *"If Julia buys an apple that costs $3 and she hands you $4, how much change should you give her?"* If you guessed $1, then you got it right! But guess who didn't? On television, all across Canada, with their parents watching? ME! ME, THE MATH GURU!

I was so worried about getting the right answer that my heart was racing, everything felt panicky, and my brain froze. I just COULDN'T do the math in my head even though I knew how. Why am I telling you this? Because everyone freaks out sometimes. Everyone! The important thing is to discover how to get through it. When that happened, it felt like the worst thing ever.

Now I'm telling this story to you and laughing REALLY hard. It's pretty funny that I got the answer to four minus three wrong on national television. You CAN learn to use your freak-outs to get stronger and smarter too. You'll realize they don't last forever and can even make for great (and funny!) stories later.

Are you ready to ride the freak-out wave? Grab your surfboard, and let's go!

#1: Countdown Let's say you're in the middle of a test and you start panicking because you can't figure something out.

1. STOP! Close your eyes. (Don't worry, no one's watching, and if they are, they probably wish they knew your mysterious Jedi ways.)
2. Take a slow breath in. Say "ten" in your head.
3. Let your breath out slowly, while silently saying "nine."
4. Continue counting down on each inhale and exhale until you get to "one."
5. Open your eyes, shake out your hands and wrists, and get back to work!

#2: Sweat it out! Having a super-stressful homework session? Nothing shakes out stress like getting sweaty. So, get up, blast your fave song, and dance your butt off! Or do ten jumping jacks AND ten push-ups AND ten sit-ups. Or get outside and run around the block. Feel better now? Of course you do! Exercise improves your mood. Your brain might not be a muscle, but it works waaayyy better after a blast of oxygen.

#3: Meditate Meditating TOTALLY helps me deal with freak-outs and it's EASY! Meditating regularly may actually help your brain deal with stress better all the time. Try it for just five or six minutes a few times a week. It can help you find your chill whenever you need it! Here are two of my favourites: the Big Red Balloon and the Big Blue Sky. They both start the same:

1. First, pick three or four days a week that you're going to commit to meditating. Make a promise to yourself and stick to it!

2. Choose a super special place to be your meditation zone. This can be a spot in your room, a couch, your bed — whatever! Every time you meditate, do it in this special spot.

3. Set a timer for FIVE little minutes. As you get used to meditating, you can add another minute or two.

4. Close your eyes. Relax your body and begin to take deep breaths in and out through your nose.

Now pick either the Big Red Balloon OR the Big Blue Sky. Go for it!

The Big Red Balloon:

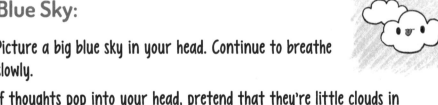

1. Take a slow, deep breath to fill your belly with air, as if you're trying to blow up a big red balloon. Expand your belly as much as you can!

2. Slowly let the air out of the imaginary balloon through your nose. Release alllll the air. All of it! You can even make a hisssss noise, just like letting air out of a real balloon.

3. Keep filling your balloon with air and letting it out, over and over, until your timer goes off.

The Big Blue Sky:

1. Picture a big blue sky in your head. Continue to breathe slowly.

2. If thoughts pop into your head, pretend that they're little clouds in your big blue sky. Don't focus on them or shove them away, just let them float by.

3. Keep thinking of your sky until your time is done.

Whenever you get stressed out or feel panicky in the middle of doing a test or homework, think about your big blue sky or breathe into your big red balloon.

#4: Get excited! Getting excited about freaking out might seem like the last thing you should do — but it's actually not! Being nervous when you're about to write a test or speak in class or do something you care about is TOTALLY NORMAL. Top athletes feel nervous all the time. They know it means they're super excited to try, and they use the adrenalin to run faster and jump higher. You can use that feeling to help you too! Be excited about the fact that you have important stuff happening, stuff you care about! Things would be pretty blah if you didn't.

#5: Get creative Did you know I'm in a rock band? I love singing, playing keytar and being on stage! But one of the BEST things is writing songs. I write about what makes me sad, or mad, or worried. I always feel better when I do something creative with the uncomfortable feelings I have. Next time you're stressed out, find a different way to express it. Draw a picture, write a story, make a collage, build a sculpture, invent a dance . . . whatever! Channel your freak-out into something creative — you may even have tons of fun with it.

#6: Talk it out One of the yuckiest parts about being overwhelmed is feeling like you're all alone and that no one understands. But I promise that's not true! Everyone feels stressed out sometimes. Talking about it makes a big huge situation feel a whole lot smaller and less scary. If things start to feel like too much to handle, talk to someone: a parent, a friend, your favourite teacher, your auntie, a guidance counsellor, even your cat! Just saying stuff out loud will help you feel better, and the person you talk to may have ways to really help. So don't be shy, give talking a try.

#7: Make a worry box If you get random worries that pop into your head — especially when you're trying to fall asleep! — you're just like me. So make a worry box for them! Decorate an empty tissue box with happy things, like cool stickers, pics, quotes and comics. Every time a worry pops into your head, write it down on a piece of paper, say "I'm going to let this thought GO for now" and stuff it in your worry box. POOF! Let the worry go from your head into the box. Later, when you are feeling good, go through the worry box. Separate your notes into two piles: things you aren't so worried about anymore and things that you are. You can chuck your "not worried" pile into the recycling. Talk to someone you trust about the "still worried" things. I'll bet that pile is probably way smaller than you thought in the first place!

#8: Be a thought detective Worrying is your brain's way of protecting you from danger. But sometimes your brain can blow up a little worry into something that feels like a wayyy bigger deal than it actually is. The thing is this: feelings ARE NOT facts! You need to play detective and figure out if those worries are a real thing to pay attention to OR just a feeling thing. One of my favourite ways to do this is called the three Cs or CA-CO-CHA. This is how it works:

1. CA! CAtch your thoughts: Imagine all the worries you have floating above your head in bubbles, like a cartoon. Now catch one. Here's one I used to have all the time: "I'm bad at everything in math class."

2. CO! COllect evidence: Now it's detective time! Collect evidence that this worry is true as well as any evidence that it is false. For example:

   True: "I failed last week's quiz on coordinates."
   False: "I looked at the questions where I lost marks, and I know what I did wrong."
   False: "I helped a friend understand the difference between a cone and a triangular prism today."
   False: "I memorized all my times tables last year. They're easy now!"

3. CHA! CHAllenge your thoughts: Now this is where the real detective work comes in. Look at all the evidence you collected. Is that worry really 100% true? Chances are it isn't. But hey, YOU be the judge!

#9: Turn WHAT IF into WHAT IS We humans are capable of time travel . . . *in our minds!* In fact, we sometimes spend A LOT of time in the future, worrying about stuff that MIGHT happen. A typical worry time traveller spends a lot of time wondering things like "What if I get the answer wrong when I put my hand up — and everyone laughs at me?" or "What if my birthday party is awkward?" The thing is, worrying about make-believe things means you're missing out on what's happening RIGHT NOW! So, when you find yourself living in the "what if," I want you to take a big breath in, let it out, and bring yourself back to the "what is"! What IS ACTUALLY happening right NOW? No one is laughing at wrong answers in class. You are literally sitting with all your BFFs at lunch, having a blast. You are wearing your favourite hoodie. All is well. Stay in the present — it's a gift!

#10: Feelings aren't forever This is my best bit of advice for hacking your chill! Can you remember the last time you felt super sad? So excited you could barely sleep? So angry you thought you would explode? Having so much fun that it was the BEST day ever? How long did any of those feelings last? Feelings come and go — even the ones that aren't so good. So when you're having a terrible day, try to remember it WON'T last forever.

GETTING UNSTUCK

What to do next when you don't know what to do next!

Have you ever tried to open a jar but no matter HOW HARD you try, the lid won't budge? When that happens to me, I have certain go-to moves: I run the jar under hot water, I put on a rubber glove for super non-slip grip, or I use the back of a spoon to tap the lid. Well, math is like that jar. There are tricks you can use to pop things open. When I can't figure out how to solve a math problem or go blank on a test, I reach for these tools to get unstuck. Remember, it's normal to feel stumped — that's a part of learning something new. Sometimes all you need is a little nudge to get your math brain loosened up!

#1: Call a friend If you're super stuck on a homework question, help is just a phone call away! Your WHOLE CLASS has to do the same question, so someone will probably know what's going on. Call a friend and ask them to explain things. Talk it out! Sometimes you just need to hear someone else explain it for things to start making sense.

#2: Get the picture Are you the type of person who learns better if you can picture it — like, with an actual picture? A lot of kids are! If that's you, just start drawing stuff. Read what your question is saying and see if you can turn it into something visual. Make a diagram, sketch a shape or use different colours to organize the info from the question. Being able to visualize things might just make a light bulb go on in your brain!

#3: Be a detective It can feel really frustrating to get stuck on a math question at home. But there's a BIG chance the clues to solving it are somewhere close — like in your backpack! Dig out your textbook, worksheets and notes from class and have a closer look. Usually teachers give you questions based on what they taught in class. The help you need might be RIGHT THERE. Look for a question like the one you're stuck on and see if you can find any hints about how to solve it. You got this, Sherlock!

#4: Make a math sundae Stay with me here! When you make a sundae, first you scoop in the ice cream. Then you put on the hot fudge sauce. Then the nuts and toppings. Then the whipped cream. And THEN the cherry. Without the ice-cream foundation at the bottom, the whole thing falls apart! Math is like that too. Let's say you're trying to do long division, but you forget your multiplication facts. They're the foundation! It would be very hard for you to do that division question without knowing them. You may need to hit the pause button on your current topic and relearn some lessons from previous units or even from your previous year. Get some help with those, then get ready to build the best math sundae EVER!

#5: Ask your fave teacher If you're feeling stumped, asking your fave teacher is SUCH a great idea because they are actual experts in explaining things. If your teacher isn't around to ask right away, circle the question or put a sticky note next to it so you can easily find it when you do get a chance to talk to them. If you're feeling scared, don't worry. Teachers are there TO HELP YOU! Asking questions lets them know that you care and want to learn, and that's music to a teacher's ears!

#6: Talk it out! If you just can't understand how to do a question, speak out! Pretend you're explaining it to your BFF or grab a stuffie and give it a mini math lesson. Read the question out loud and just start talking! What is it asking you to do, in your OWN words? What are some things that come to mind that can help you start solving the problem? What are some things you've already tried, and why didn't they work? You might find that a new idea pops into your head. Use YOUR voice and let it lead the way!

#7: Get up — literally You may not believe me, but sometimes doing math while you're standing up CHANGES EVERYTHING. Stand-up desks are totally a thing! Try working at the kitchen counter or ask an adult to help you build a raised area on your desk. Or skip the desk and tape the biggest piece of paper you can find to a wall so that you can write on it. You can even next-level it by jogging on the spot while rocking your math questions.

#8: Highlight the way Highlighters are one of my FAVOURITE math tools! Sometimes you might get stuck on figuring out what a question is asking you to do. Use your highlighters for key words and numbers in the question. Now see if you can figure out what the relationship between those words and numbers is! Using different colours might help you see what numbers go with what words in the question. Have a few highlighters in your pencil case at all times so you can pull 'em out whenever you need to!

#9: Thumbs-up for screen time Even if you have a great teacher, sometimes you might need a little extra help understanding a math lesson. The internet is there to help! There are a TON of videos, worksheets and pictures about every single math topic out there. There are also a TON of questions in case you want to get really, REALLY good with extra practice. Ask an adult to help you get online, type your math question into a search engine, and watch the magic unfold!

MEMORY HACKS

Yes, you CAN memorize anything, any time, anywhere!

I TOTALLY get it — memorizing stuff isn't always fun! But there are ways to make it a lot easier. And once you memorize all your basic facts, math becomes a LOT easier. Why? Because you can use ALL your brain power on learning new stuff and solving problems instead of trying to figure out what 3 x 7 is, like, every single time. Those facts become part of your brain's tool box, and once you have them, it takes ZERO ENERGY to use them. Try as many of these hacks as it takes. Something WILL work for you!

#1: Make a tip sheet It's a piece of paper where you write down all the math facts, steps and formulas that you need to know. Your tip sheet might contain secret legends, made-up words, drawings, diagrams and tricks that only YOU understand. Make one after the end of a unit, or to study for a test. Get it ALL together in one place and study off that. If you do, at the end of the year you'll have your own secret stash of custom notes with EVERYTHING you learned already.

#2: Step-by-step One of the best ways to memorize math formulas is by breaking them down into steps! Take any formula that's bugging you and say it out loud, in your own words, s l o w l y. Next, write down each thing you said, in order. Voila! Those are your new steps. If you wanna get fancy, you can make a poster (decorated, of course) with your steps written out so that you can see them EVERY day!

#3: Sleep on it Can you memorize math facts in your SLEEP? Well, kind of. Sometimes you'll be trying sooo hard to learn and it's like your brain just . . . can't . . . do it. But then the next morning — POOF — that thing is in your head? Well, if you're tired, it's hard for your brain to soak up the info you're trying to put in there. Also, while you are sleeping, your brain actually joins memories together and packs them neatly away so you can find them. So, when in doubt, get some sleep. You just might be surprised to see that your hard work — plus a few zzzzz's — paid off after all!

#4: Play hide and repeat One of the best ways to remember something is to keep seeing it over and over and OVER again. Write the formulas or facts you need to know on colourful sticky notes. Now hide those sticky notes all over the place. Stick 'em on your mirror, on the back of your phone, in your sock drawer, even on your fave stuffie. Then each time you run into a note, read it OUT LOUD. Before you know it, you'll have all your notes memorized. Replace them with new ones to learn even more math stuff!

Area of a parallelogram!
$A = b * h$

#5: Make up your own math language Sometimes you have a math rule to remember and it's just, like, SO hard to memorize! You can invent a new word or phrase to help you remember. Here's how:

Invent a word It doesn't have to be a real word. I use "ryf" to remind myself to reduce your fractions. I imagine a barking dog when I'm working on them. Ryf, ryf!

Invent a phrase Funny phrases help me remember things. Take coordinate order, which is always x, y. Try: candy is xtra yummy! Cacti are xtremely yowchie! Make up something easy to remember and share it with your friends so they can learn it too.

#6: Be a rockstar Okay, you know how songs will get stuck in your head without you even TRYING to memorize them? That's why I love using them to remember stuff. Think about the alphabet — you learned it BY SINGING A SONG. Take one of your favourites and change the words so that they're all about whatever it is you have to memorize.

#7: Repeat after me Guys, I know it sucks sometimes, but there's no way around it: repeating stuff over and over is the BEST possible way to get something to stick in your head. BUT there are ways to make repetition less boring! Set a timer and see how many times you can write the 8 times table over and over in five minutes — it's JUST five minutes of your life, no big deal! Write your volume and area formulas down ten times in a row, but in a different colour each time! Get out your markers and make a flash card game for shapes. Play it with your friends! There are SO many ways to practise something over and over without being bored. Get creative and you'll be surprised at how quickly you memorize those formulas and math facts!

#8: Jump around! Sometimes when it feels like your brain isn't working, it's a sign that you need to move it, move it! Stand up, do some jumping jacks, go for a jog or walk, dance super fast to your fave song — get your body flowing! Then grab a glass of water, sit down, and try again. You'll be surprised at how a little exercise goes a long way when you're studying!

#9: Use it or lose it! No matter what memory hack works for you, there's one REALLY important thing to remember: you've got to keep practising. If you trained for a race every day for a year and then stopped a month before the big meet, would your muscles still be at their best? No! With language, we remember new words by using them regularly so they stay in our brains. Math is the same. To help things stick, FULLY write out those formulas and math facts when you're doing homework. Even if you think you can do them in your head, WRITE THEM DOWN ANYWAY. And then go back and practise later. Like, if on Monday you totally have your 5 times table memorized — great! Just make sure you go over it again on Friday to be positive it's STILL in there.

MOTIVATION HACKS

For when you just don't want to . . . but you HAVE to.

Ever get that feeling where you just . . . don't . . . want . . . to . . . do . . . ANYTHING? I know I do. Sometimes when I have a big pile of work, I think about how I'd rather be doing something fun instead. But the truth is, you just have to sit down and DO THE WORK. And if you do, you'll feel SO much better! If you do your work first, playtime will be even more fun! You'll feel like you really earned it. And here's a secret: the sooner you get to whatever it is you don't want to do, the sooner you'll be DONE. You ready?!

#1: Train like an athlete It can seem like homework is pointless. But here's the thing: everyone deals with boring stuff. Top athletes practise boring stuff over and over. It helps them win races and land triple Axels. Nobody just throws themselves in the air and does a backflip with ZERO practice! It takes hours, months, YEARS of squats and practice and training . . . but that's what it takes to do the big stuff. Homework is like that too, but for your brain. Sometimes you need to do a hundred long division problems, or write your times tables fifty times in a row. But you're building your math muscles just like an athlete builds their leg muscles. You ARE getting stronger, you just might not be able to see it — YET!

#2: Reward yourself Just like you set aside "homework time" every day, set aside "reward time." Celebrate doing that math homework you TOTALLY didn't feel like doing, but did. Use your time to call your BFF, play outside or watch your favourite vids, whatever feels fun! Setting official "reward time" will give you something to get excited about!

#3: Find your why Feeling unmotivated to study? Too low in energy for that homework? Take FIVE minutes and write down your top THREE reasons for doing it. "I want to get a better mark than last time." "I want to be proud of myself." "I want to show my frenemies that I'm smarter than they think I am." Put your note where you can see it every single day. When you start thinking "This is so pointless!" or "Why am I even bothering?" LOOK AT YOUR NOTE and give yourself a motivational boosty-boost!

#4: Shake it UP When things feel boring, SPICE IT UP! That means doing the things you have to do, but in a fun and different way. Do your homework on the balcony or in the backyard. Plan a unicorn study party. Try three practice questions right after breakfast. Wear your Halloween costume while studying. Work on a project while listening to your fave music and taking dance breaks. Do all your homework in different colours. Get weird, get wacky, and watch your motivation go from zero to SUPERHERO!

#5: Mmm . . . Cake! You know how cake tastes EXTRA yummy because it's only a sometimes treat? Well, that's how I think about free time. If you never had ANY work to do and it was just cake ALL the time, 24-7, you would start getting tired of it. And no one wants to be bored of cake! Treat your homework like fruits and veggies, and treat your free time like CAKE. If you eat those fruits and veggies, you might find you actually like some of them! Then you can go and totally enjoy a bit of cake, and it'll taste EVEN SWEETER!

#6: Convince yourself Hey, you! Yes, YOU! It's time to stop telling yourself that you don't wanna! One of my absolute fave expressions is "what you focus on grows." It means that the more you think about feeling bad, the worse you will feel. But the good news is that it works in reverse too. The more you focus on feeling POSITIVE, the HAPPIER you will feel! So, change that channel! Instead of thinking "OMG, ew, I hate this, I'm bored," try "This isn't so bad, this is kind of fun, I feel GREAT ABOUT MYSELF FOR DOING ALL THIS HARD WORK RIGHT NOW, YAY!" It might sound silly, but trust me — it works! Before you know it, you'll see that you can change your mindset by changing your thoughts. What you focus on grows, so start focusing on the POSITIVE.

#7: Find your cheerleaders Even a super-positive person can need a little help to get out of a funk and back to their funky-fun self! And what better way to do it than a personal cheer squad? Make a list of people you can call on when you're feeling low. This might include your favourite auntie, your oldest brother, your BFF or anyone that you know is on TEAM YOU. Tack that list to your wall. Next time you're feeling bummed about school, call someone on your list and tell them you need some encouragement! Surround yourself with as many positive people as you can. You'll notice that YOU will start feeling their good vibes too.

#8: Be your own pen pal Everyone has good patches and bad ones. When you're in a good mood, write your future "grumpy self" a letter! Think about what you would say to a friend who's down on their work because they're bored or sad. How would you cheer them up and get them going? Start by writing Dear [your name!] . . . and let your pep talk FLOW. Throw a few stickers or doodles on there, stuff it in an envelope addressed to yourself and stash it in a special spot. Next time you're feeling blah about homework, open that letter and give it a read. You just became your very own pen pal pep talker!

It's OK!

#9: Ready . . . set . . . GO!

When I'm feeling like I TOTALLY don't want to do something, instead of thinking about how much I don't want to do it, I just make myself START. Once I get going, that thing I totally didn't want to do isn't as bad as I thought it would be. And after a few minutes things start feeling easier and more fun. So, if you're not inspired at first, don't worry about it — just get started. The motivation will catch up with YOU!

#10: Start a homework club

Have an assignment you REALLY don't want to do? I bet a few of your friends from school ALSO have that assignment and ALSO don't really want to do it! When I was in school, my super-fun club got me through tests, homework and projects. The four of us did our homework together at someone's house if we could, and if we couldn't, we'd call each other when we needed help. My homework club was my fave part of school. You can start one by inviting a few of your friends or classmates who make you feel good about yourself!

PRODUCTIVITY HACKS
Some help for when you need to get stuff DONE!

"Productivity" is a big word that adults LOVE using — a lot. Basically, it means "getting stuff done"! The thing you need to know is that being productive actually feels good. REALLY GOOD! It's a satisfied feeling that you can ONLY get by getting things done. Think about a time when you finished a big project, completed a game or (finally) cleaned your room. Those things probably seemed big and intimidating at first. But once you finished them . . . how good did you feel? Pretty great, right? Everyone struggles with this — even adults. But I'm about to teach YOU some great ways to get stuff DONE.

#1: You do you I'm a morning person. I LOVE getting up early! But if I don't go to bed early, I get so cranky that I have a name for it: the night sads! Nighttime is NOT a good time for me to do work. That means that I HAVE to finish it in the daytime so that at night I can relax, read a book, and go to bed early. What time of day are YOU most able to concentrate, focus and do work? It's probably when you're feeling alert and happy. Plan to do your school work then. Just like that, you've hacked your day and found the perfect time to get into your signature study zone!

#2: Un-distract yourself! One of the biggest things that can get in the way of getting things done — especially homework — is getting distracted! There are a LOT of things that can distract us: phones, pets, siblings, sounds around the house and even the thoughts inside our heads! To stay focused, find a quiet place to work. Get rid of anything that might distract you. That means putting away books or toys, closing your computer, and DEFINITELY putting away your screens (tablet, phone, whatever) so that you can't even SEE them. Let people (siblings, grown-ups, friends) know that you are about to get stuff done and ask them nicely to please not bug you unless it's SUPER important. Start getting stuff done!

#3: Break it down Sometimes a BIG project can seem so huge that it's impossible to even know where to start! So here's how to begin: just break it down. Take out a sheet of paper and break your BIG project into a list of mini-projects that don't seem so scary. Schedule time to complete each of the minis, and guess what? Once you're done all those little tiny projects, your big project will be totally DONE! I did that when I wrote this book! It seemed scary to write a whole big book, but then I broke the book down into chapters (like the one you're reading right now!), and it seemed so much easier. One by one, I finished each chapter and — voila! — I had a book. This book that you are actually holding in your hands right now!

#4: Focus pocus! Staying focused can be hard. There's a lot of exciting stuff going on in the world! But there's a magic device that can help: a timer! By breaking your work AND your time down into smaller chunks, it's easier to stay focused. When it's time for homework, set a timer for twenty minutes and get to work. No matter what, don't give up. Do as much work as you can, and when you hear the "BING," you get a break. Breaks are SO IMPORTANT! Your brain needs breaks when it's concentrating hard. Make a snack, lift some weights, sit and daydream (my favourite!). Set the timer for five minutes and go do whatever you want. When your time is up, back to work! Set it again for — you guessed it — another twenty minutes. Reset and repeat. You'll have your homework done in no time!

* Get a stopwatch or an egg timer, or use your alarm clock. Anything that can let you know when time's up.

* Download an app. I use a timer app on my phone that you can set intervals on. BUT always put your phone on airplane mode while you're working so you don't get distracted.

* Don't look at your timer! No matter which timer you choose, no sneaking peeks at how much time is left. Set your timer, get to work, and take a break when it goes off.

* If twenty minutes is too much at first, no biggie. Try ten or fifteen to get into the groove.

#5: Make a list and check it twice! Sometimes it feels like there are a MILLION things to do and they're all swimming around your head. As soon as you start doing ONE thing, all the OTHER things keep jumping in and you just can't concentrate. The best way to organize the thoughts in your head is to make a TO-DO LIST. Sit down and write out ALL the things you have to do. Maybe that's homework, projects, a test you need to study for, music practice, chores, whatever. You can even have "Make to-do list" on your list! Now that it's all written out on a piece of paper, take a deep breath and exhale. Cross "Make to-do list" off your list. Don't you feel better already?

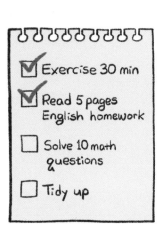

#6: Put your "binoculars" on Well, some pretend ones, anyway. Everything looks so much closer now, right? Treat your homework and studying that way. When teachers assign tests and projects weeks into the future, it can feel sooo far away. Like, you don't even need to THINK about it yet. But time FLIES, and before you know it, your project is due or it's test day. Scrambling at the last minute is stressful, and it's hard to do a good job! Put on your "binoculars" so that everything seems closer than it actually is. Start working on stuff sooner than you think you have to. It's SO much better to be finished a project early rather than too late.

#7: Be your own personal assistant There's a reason celebrities and top executives have them. Personal assistants have the superpower of being scheduling MASTERS! They can turn each day into the perfect combo of getting stuff done PLUS lots of time for chillaxing. And YOU can be YOUR OWN personal assistant. Here's how:

* Get your own agenda or design one using a calendar or notebook. It helps to have something where each day is on a separate page so you have lots of room to write.

* At the beginning of each week, take your agenda out and plan your week, day by day. I like doing this on Sundays before the week even starts so I feel READY for everything when I wake up on Monday. Start by putting in the stuff you KNOW is happening each day. So, maybe block off 9:00–4:00 for school and 6:00–7:00 for dinner. Then you can see how much time you have left for other things.

* Next, block off time for school work and fun stuff! This might mean deciding on certain hours each day when you're going to do homework, dedicating specific chunks of time for screens, snacks and meeting up with friends, and finding time slots to work on tests or projects that are coming up. That might look like: 4:00–5:00 snacks 'n' chillax; 5:00–6:00 homework; 7:00–7:30 test review.

* Make sure you're always wearing your "binoculars" (see hack #6). Look at deadlines that are coming up in the next couple of weeks. Book time to work on those projects or study for those tests NOW. And keep your "appointments" so that you don't fall into the oops-left-it-until-the-last-minute trap.

#8: Take a time out How can NOT doing stuff help you GET it done? Trust me, it works! Your brain needs breaks when it's concentrating hard, just like your body does during a workout. If your mind starts spinning or you're starting to get cranky or hungry, take a time out. Set a timer (yay, timers!) for ten minutes and go do something completely different to clear your mind. Check in on a friend, go cuddle your cat, or put on your fave song and dance around your room. Do a little battery recharge! Once your timer goes off, sit back down and get to work. You'll be amazed at how much better your brain is working, and you'll feel pretty good too!

TEST HACKS

Yes, you CAN kill it on game day!

Do you stress about tests? If you do, YOU'RE JUST LIKE MOST KIDS! I used to HATE writing tests, but that was before I figured out some ways to make them actually kind of FUN. That's right, I said FUN! There are two parts to being a good test taker. First, you need to chill out so you can get into writing the test. You'll find great advice in the Chill-out Hacks section on page 13. Second, there's the actual strategy part. This means knowing how to be prepared and show off what you know. So, let's get into those, right here, right now!

#1: Give yourself the star treatment What does a top athlete need before game day? A good night's sleep, a healthy breakfast and lots of self-love and positive thinking! Being rested and fed and feeling good will TOTALLY help you be at the top of your math game.

#2: Play dress-up I'm serious. On test day I want you walking into class wearing whatever makes YOU feel like a total superhero! If that means you're wearing your comfiest sweats, put them on. If that means wearing a glitter top, you DO THAT. If you have to wear a uniform to school, no biggie! Stash a good-luck charm in your pocket, wear a cool button, tie a rainbow ribbon in your hair — whatever it takes to make you feel ready to KICK BUTT!

39

#3: Do a little skimmy-skim When you get your test, you could just start and do each question in order. But I recommend having a quick look at the whole test first. Then, YOU pick which question you want to start with. If you tackle what you're most confident about first, it will help you get into your math groove. If a question that stumps you, skip it and come back to it later. This will save you a lot of time — and stress! Chances are there are things on the test you know and some you don't, and that's fine. Build your mojo by nailing the easy stuff first!

#4: Take ACTUAL time with the question Sometimes you're so excited (or nervous) when writing a test that you race right through the directions. It's easy to lose marks this way. Slow down and really, REALLY read the question. Bust out that pencil case and highlight key info in the question, the numbers that you see and the keywords that give you clues about what you need to do. This will help you organize your thoughts — AND your answer — much better!

#5: Form is your friend This is a biggie! Make sure you understand exactly how your teacher wants each test question answered. If you write your answer in the wrong form, you'll lose marks. And that would be sad. If it says to round to two decimal places — DO IT! Label your x and y axes on a graph? DO IT! Remember to read the question carefully to find clues about what your answer should look like.

#6: Check your logic Yay, you answered a test question — but wait! Before moving on to the next one, double-check that your answer makes ACTUAL SENSE. This can be especially useful for word problems. Like, if Sammy has 3 cupcakes and Jack has 2, and you add them up and get 60, does that make any sense? Nope! You probably just made a calculation error. If you don't double-check, you won't be able to fix it!

#7: Sentences are super If you're solving a word problem, you HAVE to put your final answer in a FULL concluding sentence! If the question asks, "How many gumballs does Sarah have?" you can't just scribble 38 on a piece of paper. You have to ANSWER the question with words: "Sarah has 38 gumballs." When you're writing math, you're telling a story. You want the person reading it to be able to follow it. Don't skimp out on those sentences — they're worth marks, and you need them to tell your whole math story.

#8: Do a time check Feeling like you're taking too long to finish a question can be stressful. So BEFORE you start, have a look at how much each question is worth. The ones worth the most are the ones to spend the longest on. If a question is only worth, like, one mark, it shouldn't take forever — and if it does, just move on to the next one. Save your time for where it matters. Have a peek at the clock once in a while. Chances are you DO have time for everything!

#9: Fill in the blanks If you're totally stuck on a question, just chill for a moment — it happens! But then, START WRITING something. If you do, sometimes the way to figure it out will pop into your head. Plus, you'll probably get MARKS for writing stuff down, even if you can't fully answer the question. You can still write down some of the key info. Draw a diagram. Jot numbers down. Put your thoughts into words YOU understand. Never leave a question blank. EVER!

#10: Find your check-your-work zone You're gonna want to check your work, but HOW you do it is up to you. You can finish all the questions FIRST and then go back and check them. If you're in a groove, sometimes it's good to do it this way. I prefer to do each question slowly, then check JUST THAT ONE over before moving on. Then I'm not in a rush at the end, panic-changing answers that were actually right in the first place. But you need to decide what's best for you!

#11: Pay attention to the little things Sometimes during a test, you're SO focused on the big picture that you forget things like reducing final fractions, putting measurement units at the end of your numbers or answering word problems in full sentences. And those little things can add up to a lot of lost marks! Once you're done each question, hit the pause button. Make sure you've looked out for the little guys and added in those teeny details that make your answer perfecto!

#12: Learn from your mistakes I get it — the second you're done a test, you never want to see it again. But tests are awesome teaching tools. They can tell you about your "test-writing bugs," those little mistakes that lose you marks: things like being too messy, forgetting to label your units or showing your work. After you get a test back, take a good look to see where you went wrong. If you forgot a math rule, make a note and practise! Ask your teacher to help you figure out the questions you got wrong. Write down the correct answers. Bonus points for asking for a blank copy of the test and writing it again at home! This will give you a chance to really show yourself what you have learned.

#13: Be a show-off Normally I'm not into telling anyone to be a big show-off, but when it comes to math tests, I'm totally cool with it. BUT IT'S NOT ABOUT THE MARKS! The thing is, we've been thinking about tests the wrong way! We're so obsessed with getting perfect scores and not making mistakes that we've forgotten what tests are really for. They're for showing off the HARD WORK you've been doing to learn stuff. They're for showing off that all those nights spent doing homework taught you something. They're for showing off the stuff you should be PROUD to KNOW. That's it . . . that's all! Stop worrying about the marks and focus on finally celebrating all that hard work you've been doing. THAT'S what tests are for!

PART 2

HACK THE MATH!

COORDINATES
Your Personal Mathematical Treasure Map!

What even are they?! This is a kind of system that helps us describe exactly WHERE a point is. We start with a **coordinate grid**, which is sort of like a map. On the grid, we plot out points and label them with numbers. These numbers are called **coordinates**. Once you know how the system works, you can always figure out exactly where something is — just like a super-cool treasure map!

COORDINATE GRIDS

A coordinate grid is made up of evenly spaced horizontal and vertical lines that cross each other at right angles (more about those on page 57!). Those lines create perfect squares, like on graph paper. Let's take a closer look.

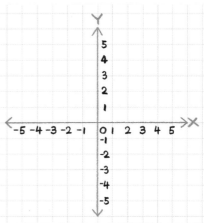

 MEMORIZE THIS!

Do you keep getting confused between horizontal and vertical and which is which? Draw an "H" and a "V." Now, have a look at "H." It has a line going left to right, so "horizontal" is the word we use to describe a flat line going totally straight left to right. And "V" has a point facing downward, so "vertical" is the word we use to describe a line that's totally straight up and down!

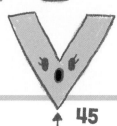

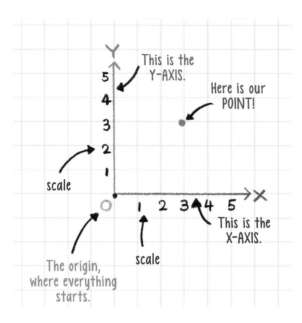

This is the Y-AXIS.

Here is our POINT!

scale

This is the X-AXIS.

scale

The origin, where everything starts.

Notice that there are two main lines on the left and the bottom of our grid. These are the most important lines — they're sort of like boundaries on a map. The horizontal line on the bottom is called the **x-axis**. We move along the x-axis left and right. The vertical line on the left is called the **y-axis**. We move along the y-axis up and down. The x-axis and y-axis act like fences on our coordinate grid. We use arrows at the end of each to show that they could go on forever and ever.

The **origin**, marked with a zero, is where BOTH x and y equal zero. The numbers on the x-axis and y-axis are kind of like a ruler; they're called the **scale**. These numbers allow us to find ANY point ANYwhere in our grid.

Points always have BOTH an x-coordinate and a y-coordinate. We write coordinates using brackets like this: (x, y). The x value is our point's x-coordinate, or where it lines up to the x-axis. The y value is our point's y-coordinate, or where it lines up to the y-axis.

MARK YOUR MAP

A map doesn't make much sense without being labelled. You'll keep track of where you are and score marks on tests by labelling every part of your coordinate grid properly.

1. Mark your x-axis with an x and your y-axis with a y.
2. Put arrows on the ends of your x and y axes.
3. Make sure your scale is clearly labelled.
4. Label the coordinates of your point (x, y), and fill in whatever the x and y values are.

If your x and y axes represent something specific (like, in a word problem), make sure you describe what they're measuring in your answer. For example, if your x-axis measures hours, and your y-axis measures doughnuts, make sure to write (6 hours, 3 doughnuts).

FINDING THE COORDINATES OF A POINT

So, how do we tell where our cool little point is by using our math treasure-map system? Let me show you! We've been given this point called A, plotted in a coordinate grid.

Q: Find the coordinates of point A.

First, it's important to know what the question is asking us to do! We're being asked to find both the x and y coordinates of point A so that we can describe where that point is on our grid!

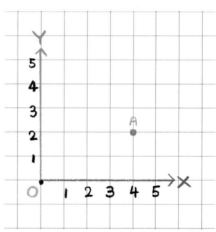

47

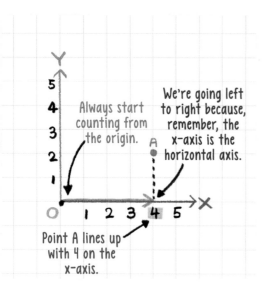

We're going left to right because, remember, the x-axis is the horizontal axis.

Always start counting from the origin.

Point A lines up with 4 on the x-axis.

Step 1: To find the coordinates of A, first find out how many squares along the x-axis you need to go to get directly below A. Always start at the origin — which is at zero! Remember, the x-axis is horizontal, which means you move left to right, NOT up and down! Count squares along the x-axis until you see that you're lined up with your point. Count 4 squares and your x-coordinate is 4!

Step 2: Then, figure out what your y-coordinate is. This time, read UP the y-axis to see how many squares it takes to get to the point. Count 2 squares up from the origin, so your y-coordinate is 2!

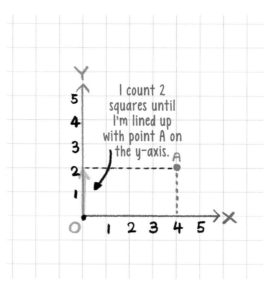

I count 2 squares until I'm lined up with point A on the y-axis.

Step 3: Now, it's time to label your point. Remember, a coordinate is labelled (x, y), with the x-coordinate going first and the y-coordinate second — JUST like their order in the alphabet! So, the point's coordinates are (4, 2), which means 4 squares to the right and 2 squares up! You're done!

A: The coordinates of point A are (4, 2).

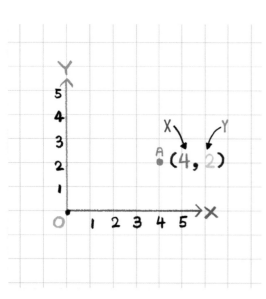

X   Y

A (4, 2)

PLOTTING A COORDINATE ON YOUR MAP

Okay, now what about when you have to plot your own coordinate on your math map? Well, it's SUPER easy now that you know how the coordinate grid works!

Q: Plot the point whose coordinates are (5, 2) on your grid.

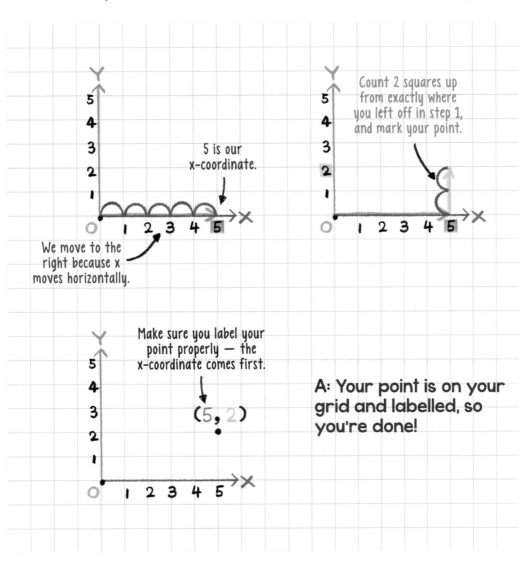

5 is our x-coordinate.

We move to the right because x moves horizontally.

Count 2 squares up from exactly where you left off in step 1, and mark your point.

Make sure you label your point properly — the x-coordinate comes first.

(5, 2)

A: Your point is on your grid and labelled, so you're done!

COORDINATE ABCs

When you're plotting points, make sure to pay special attention to the order of your coordinates. It matters! You can remember it with your ABCs. X comes before y in the alphabet, so it makes sense that we label our coordinates (x, y) with the x before the y! X comes first and moves horizontally. Y comes second and moves vertically. Got it? Watch this!

Both points have a 2 AND a 5 in them, BUT pay close attention . . .

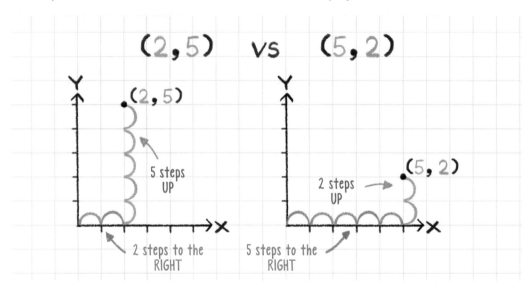

In our first example, the 2 comes first, which means it's in the x spot. And the 5 comes second, which means it's in the y spot.

In our second example, the 5 comes first, which means it's in the x spot. And the 2 comes second, which means it's in the y spot.

Expanding the Treasure Map: Negative Coordinates and Quadrants

There's just one little thing to add to what you know. Ready? Negative coordinates are a thing! But there is no need to panic. So far we've been looking at one quarter of a real-life coordinate grid. The full-size grid looks like a giant plus sign. Deep breath . . . if you see one, you got this!

When we extend the x and y axes beyond the origin point, (0, 0), we create four different sections, called **quadrants**! Here's what they look like:

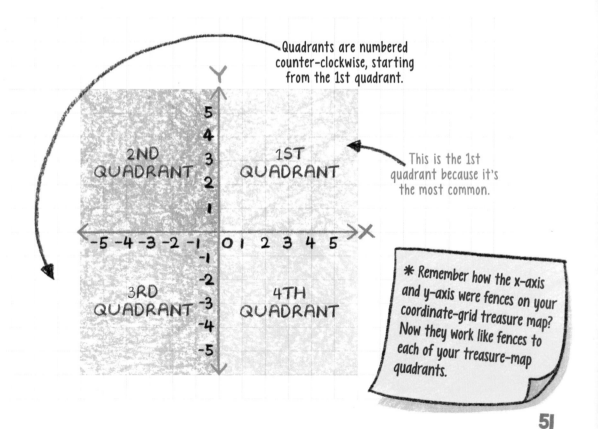

Quadrants are numbered counter-clockwise, starting from the 1st quadrant.

2ND QUADRANT

1ST QUADRANT

This is the 1st quadrant because it's the most common.

3RD QUADRANT

4TH QUADRANT

* Remember how the x-axis and y-axis were fences on your coordinate-grid treasure map? Now they work like fences to each of your treasure-map quadrants.

NEGATIVE AND POSITIVE COORDINATES

The x and y axes work like number lines. Once you go left or down past zero, you're in negative-number territory. So, points can have positive coordinates, negative coordinates or a mixture of both! It all depends on WHICH quadrant your point is in. Remember, you know how to plot a point and how to read the coordinates of a point. NONE of this changes when you move into other quadrants, so don't overthink it!

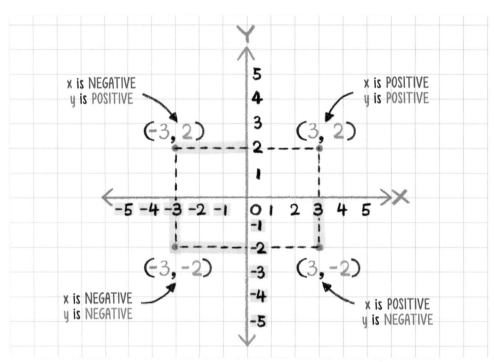

1st quadrant: Look at your point. If you make a dotted line connecting it to the x-axis, you'll see that it lines up with 3 (make sure your line runs along the grid lines, not diagonally). If you make a dotted line connecting your point to the y-axis (make sure your line runs along the grid lines, not diagonally), you can see that it lines up with 2. So, your coordinates are (3, 2), which are BOTH POSITIVE.

2nd quadrant: Now, let's do the same thing here. Make your dotted lines, and just see what you hit! You've lined up with –3 on the x-axis and 2 on the y-axis, so your coordinates are (–3, 2). If your point is anywhere in this quadrant, x will be negative and y will be positive.

3rd quadrant: Again! That dotted line from your point to the x-axis now gives you –3, and the dotted line from your point to the y-axis gives you –2. Our coordinates are (–3, –2). This is the only quadrant where BOTH coordinates are always NEGATIVE!

4th quadrant: One last time with those dotted lines! From your point to the x-axis, you hit 3. From your point to the y-axis, we hit –2. Your coordinates are (3, –2). In this quadrant, x is always positive and y is always negative!

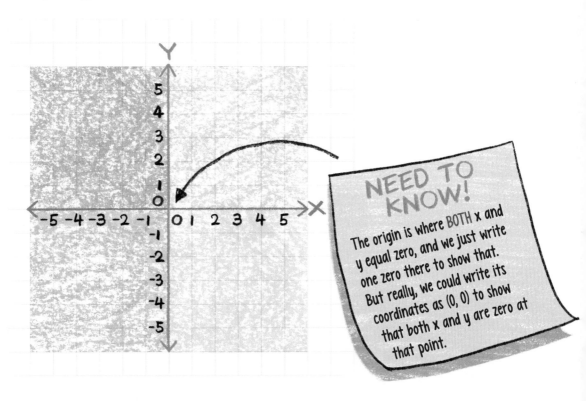

NEED TO KNOW!

The origin is where BOTH x and y equal zero, and we just write one zero there to show that. But really, we could write its coordinates as (0, 0) to show that both x and y are zero at that point.

LINES

Straight Up — Let's Do This!

What even are they?! In the world of math, a **line** has no thickness and goes on forever and ever. A line also has no end — and no beginning. What we are USUALLY talking about when we say "line" is **line segment**, which joins two points together. A line segment has ends. It's good to know the difference.

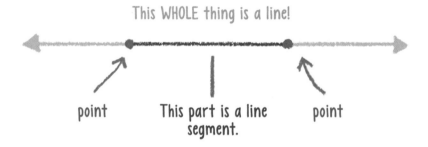

This WHOLE thing is a line!

point

This part is a line segment.

point

A **point** has no length, width or thickness, and we usually show one with a dot or an x. We can describe EXACTLY where a point is in space by using a coordinate system — more on that in the previous chapter! You need two points to make a line segment.

A line segment is that purple part marked by points on either side.

The arrows on the ends of the green line show that it keeps going in both directions.

Different Kinds of Lines

Lines can go in all kinds of directions. But some lines are special, and you need to know them!

HORIZONTAL LINES

Horizontal lines are perfectly straight from left to right, AND they line up with the horizon — that's how I like to remember their name. Horizontal lines are 100% level. Think of a shelf — if it was slanted, everything would slide off! If we drew a line across a shelf, it would be a horizontal line!

A horizontal line is parallel to the horizon and is level from LEFT to RIGHT.

VERTICAL LINES

Vertical lines are perfectly straight up and down. Think of a skyscraper — if it didn't go straight up and down, it would fall over! If we drew a line up and down a building, it would be a vertical line. If your line is slanty at all, then it's not a vertical or horizontal line.

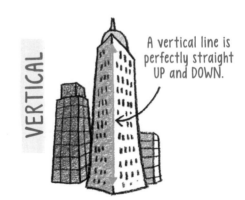

A vertical line is perfectly straight UP and DOWN.

The most important thing about lines is that they are PERFECTLY STRAIGHT. Don't bother with shortcuts — use a ruler! They're literally MADE for drawing lines. Trust me, it makes a huge difference and will probably score you extra marks on your next test.

SLANT LINES

All of the lines in the world that aren't horizontal or vertical are **slant lines**. You can also call a slant line an **oblique line** if you want to impress your friends.

SLANT

Even though this line is straight, it slants, so it isn't horizontal. It's SLANT!

SLANT

Even though this line is straight, it slants, so it isn't horizontal. It's SLANT!

WATCH OUT!

Sometimes people call slant lines, "diagonal lines." But they are NOT the same! In geometry, a diagonal is a line segment on the inside of a shape that joins two corners that aren't next to each other.

PARALLEL LINES

When two or more lines are exactly the same distance from one another, like, the whole way along, we call them **parallel lines**! Parallel lines never meet, no matter how long they are. They're like long-lost friends who live across the world from one another.

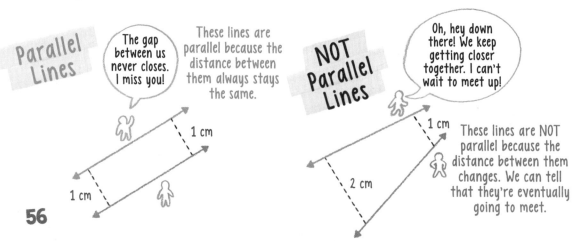

Parallel Lines

The gap between us never closes. I miss you!

These lines are parallel because the distance between them always stays the same.

1 cm

1 cm

NOT Parallel Lines

Oh, hey down there! We keep getting closer together. I can't wait to meet up!

1 cm

2 cm

These lines are NOT parallel because the distance between them changes. We can tell that they're eventually going to meet.

PERPENDICULAR LINES

Perpendicular lines are also like friends, but ones that are racing towards one another! These lines always come in pairs. When the two perpendicular lines meet, or have the chance to meet, it's always at a **right angle**.

Perpendicular Lines

These lines are perpendicular because they're headed straight for each other at a 90° angle.

Hey! I'm heading over. See you soon!

Perpendicular

We use this square symbol to mark a right angle.

These lines meet at a right angle, so they're perpendicular!

Yup! Still Perpendicular

These lines are also perpendicular, even though they're on a slant!

ALSO Perpendicular

Even though these lines don't actually meet on this diagram, we know that lines extend forever, so we can see that if we drew them longer, they would form a right angle. That means they're perpendicular to each other!

Still Perpendicular

These lines meet at a right angle, so they're also perpendicular!

Fancy Lingo!

Lines that cross each other are also called **intersecting lines**. The point where they cross is called the **point of intersection**. Think of it like a road intersection!

LENGTH

The Long and the Short of It!

What even is it?! **Length** is the shortest distance from one point to another. Seriously, that's all it is!

This little dot here is a point! Let's call her A.

And this other teeny dot over here is another point!

Let's call him B.

And here's the length — from point A to point B!

Watch out for these keywords! If you see these magic words, they're probably talking about measuring length.

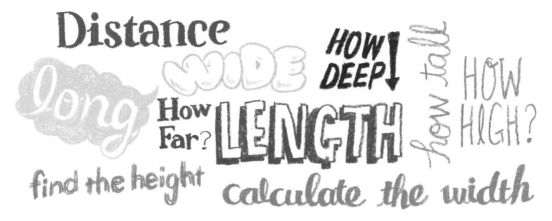

Distance WIDE HOW DEEP! how tall HOW HIGH? long How Far? LENGTH find the height calculate the width

Height is usually measured from the ground up, like how tall a building is. We're just talking about the LENGTH of that height!

Distance measures how far apart two things are. Think of the distance between your place and where your BFF lives! We're just talking about the LENGTH of that distance!

Width is usually measured from side to side, like the width of a door. It's just the LENGTH of that width!

Depth is usually measured downward, when we're thinking about how deep something is. For example, think of the depth of the ocean! So, here we're talking about the LENGTH of that depth.

Measuring Length

How do we measure length? In Canada, length is measured in **metric** units, a system of measuring things that most of the world uses as well. Metric is a very cool system because everything works on base 10 (more on that later). Here are the basic (and most popular!) metric units you need to know for measuring length.

Millimetres: This unit is used for measuring teeny-tiny things, like how long an ant is. One millimetre is about the thickness of a pencil lead. Short form: **mm**

Centimetres: These are great for measuring small, but not teeny, things, like how wide a chocolate bar is. One centimetre is about the width of your fingernail. Short form: **cm**

Metres: Use this unit for measuring kind-of-big things, like how tall you are or even how tall your school is! One metre is about the length of a guitar. Short form: **m**

Kilometres: If the distance is very big, you're going to want to use kilometres, like for measuring the distance between your place and your fave ice-cream shop. One kilometre is about the distance you can travel by walking for ten minutes. Short form: **km**

Length in ACTION!

CONVERTING BETWEEN UNITS OF LENGTH

We can change all of the units of length into one another. I know that sounds confusing, but it's actually really cool! The small units all "fit" into the units that are bigger than them by multiples of 10. All you have to do is multiply or divide by multiples of 10 to get from one unit to another. This is how a base 10 system works. By playing hopscotch left to right or right to left, you can easily convert between all of these units!

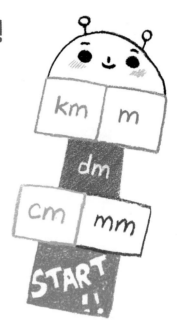

From BIG units to SMALL units: *multiply*

x 10   x 10   x 10   x 10   x 10   x 10

Official name	kilometre	hectometre	decametre	metre	decimetre	centimetre	millimetre
Short form	km	hm	dam	m	dm	cm	mm
Prefix	kilo	hecto	deca		deci	centi	milli
Metres	1000	100	10	1	1/10	1/100	1/1000

÷ 10   ÷ 10   ÷ 10   ÷ 10   ÷ 10   ÷ 10

From SMALL units to BIG units: *divide*

Hopping this way, each metric unit gets 10 times BIGGER.

Hopping this way, each metric unit gets 10 times SMALLER.

CONVERTING BETWEEN CM, M AND KM

Here's a shortcut to converting between the most popular units of length: the kilometre, the metre and the centimetre.

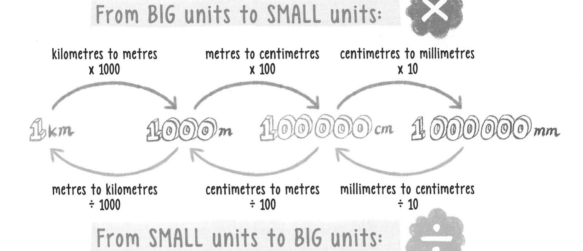

From BIG units to SMALL units: ✕

| kilometres to metres x 1000 | metres to centimetres x 100 | centimetres to millimetres x 10 |

1 km → 1000 m → 100 000 cm → 1 000 000 mm

| metres to kilometres ÷ 1000 | centimetres to metres ÷ 100 | millimetres to centimetres ÷ 10 |

From SMALL units to BIG units: ÷

DOING ACTUAL MATH WITH LENGTH!

What do we even do with length? Well, we can add, subtract, divide and multiply with length just like we do with other numbers. There's really not much to it!

Q: Your friend's ice-cream cone is 170 mm tall and yours is 20 cm tall. Who has the bigger ice cream?

To find out, we need both measurements to be in the same unit. Let's convert her mm to your cm. To do that, we just divide 170 by 10!

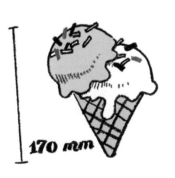

170 mm

20 cm

$$170 \div 10 = 17$$

A: 20 > 17, so your ice-cream cone wins!

 We also could have converted your cm to her mm by multiplying 20 by 10. So, 20 x 10 = 200. Since 200 > 170, you still win. The final result will be the same no matter which unit we choose to convert to!

Q: If all that ice cream was together to make one towering ice-cream cone, what would the length be if the cone part is 10 cm tall?

To find out, we need all measurements to be in the same unit. Let's convert mm to cm. To do that, we just divide 170 by 10!

$$170 \div 10 = 17$$

Now that both cone measurements are in the same units, we just add them together!

$$17 + 20 = 37$$

But wait! There's that extra cone in there. It's 10 cm tall, so let's subtract that.

$$37 - 10 = 27$$

A: The super-size ice-cream cone is 27 cm tall.

WATCH OUT!

You can't add, subtract or even compare lengths unless ALL of them are being measured using the SAME unit. Make sure you pick ONE unit to convert all of your lengths to before doing ANY actual math with your measurements.

SYSTEMS OF MEASUREMENT

Some countries use totally different units of measurement. Canada — and most of the world — uses the metric system. A couple of countries, including the United States, use the **imperial** system. If you've ever taken a road trip to the U.S., you'll notice the speed-limit signs on the highway are written in mph, which means MILES per hour! In Canada, they're written in km/h, which means KILOMETRES per hour! Cool, right?!

Here are some of the imperial units you may have come across and their conversions to the metric system.

Inches	**Feet**	Miles
1 inch = 2.54 cm	1 foot = 30.48 cm	1 mile = 1.61 km
So, 5 inches is 12.7 cm	So, 5 feet is 152.4 cm	So, 5 miles is 8.05 km
	. . . or 1.52 m	
	(see page 61 to convert cm to m!)	

ANGLES

They're around Every Corner!

What even are they?! An **angle** is the amount of turn — or rotation — between two rays that are joined at one end. So, the lines can spin around, like the hands of a clock . . . except we call them **rays** (or arms!) when we're talking about angles.

A ray is a part of a line that has a fixed starting point, but no end point — it can go on forever! Just think of a ray of sunshine! It starts in the very middle of the sun, and then shoots out into the galaxy forever. Sometimes rays are called arms. I like arms, so we're going to use that here.

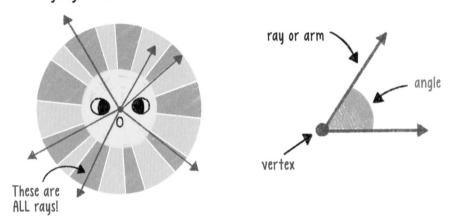

These are ALL rays!

ray or arm

angle

vertex

Angles are based on circles, so let's start with a clock ticking backwards as an example. We can think of the centre as the starting point for our first arm — the second hand in our diagram. Just picture it travelling around the clock. That's what we mean when we talk about amount of turn.

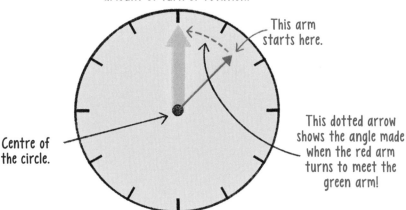

Our starting arm turns to make this angle. The movement of this arm is called the amount of turn or rotation.

This arm starts here.

Centre of the circle.

This dotted arrow shows the angle made when the red arm turns to meet the green arm!

Let's zoom in on that! Here you can see what I mean about how much you need to turn one arm so that it lies on top of the other arm:

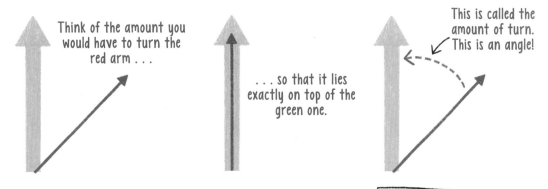

Think of the amount you would have to turn the red arm . . .

. . . so that it lies exactly on top of the green one.

This is called the amount of turn. This is an angle!

But angles aren't just inside circles — angles are EVERYWHERE! Here are just a few places where you might spot an angle.

Impress Your Friends!

If you see a little box like this drawn in the corner of a shape, it means there is a special angle there. That angle is a right angle, which is exactly 90°!

PARTS OF AN ANGLE

Now, let's REALLY get into angles! An angle is made up of three parts. It has two arms that meet at a point called the **vertex**.

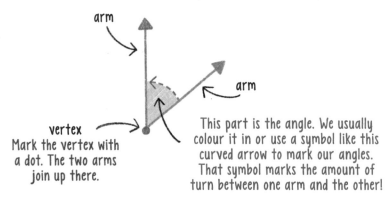

arm

arm

vertex
Mark the vertex with a dot. The two arms join up there.

This part is the angle. We usually colour it in or use a symbol like this curved arrow to mark our angles. That symbol marks the amount of turn between one arm and the other!

Degrees

How do we measure angles? We measure angles using units called **degrees**. The symbol for degrees is this little circle: °, which we place to the top right of the last digit of our number! So, 90° means "90 degrees." We usually note angles with that little degree symbol instead of writing it all out. A cool tool for measuring angles is called a **protractor** — it's like a special ruler JUST for angles.

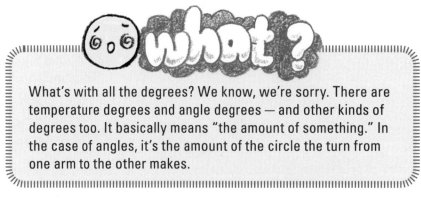

what?

What's with all the degrees? We know, we're sorry. There are temperature degrees and angle degrees — and other kinds of degrees too. It basically means "the amount of something." In the case of angles, it's the amount of the circle the turn from one arm to the other makes.

GOING FULL CIRCLE

A full sweep around a circle is 360°, but there are many stops along the way!

A quarter of a circle is 90°, known as a right angle.

Half a circle is 180°, known as a straight angle.

A full circle is 360°.

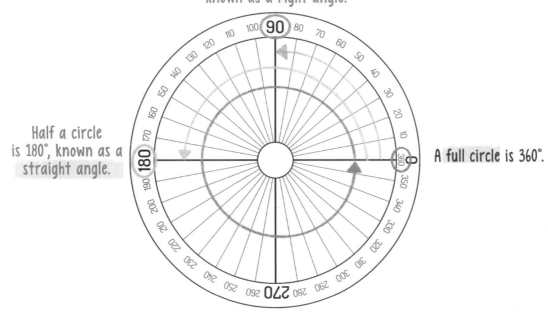

Let's have a closer look:

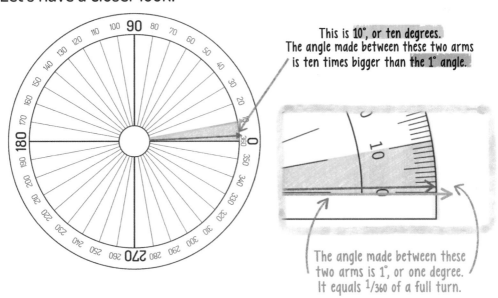

This is 10°, or ten degrees. The angle made between these two arms is ten times bigger than the 1° angle.

The angle made between these two arms is 1°, or one degree. It equals 1/360 of a full turn.

What's Your Angle?

There are lots and lots of angles out there, but here are the ones you need to know!

Acute Angle: Any angle that's less than 90°! For example, 75° is an acute angle.

Right Angle: An angle that is EXACTLY 90°!

Half Right Angle: An angle that is exactly 45°, which is half of a right angle!

Obtuse Angle: An angle that's bigger than 90° but smaller than 180°! For example, 120° is an obtuse angle.

Straight Angle: An angle that is 180°. We call this a straight angle because it looks like a straight line!

Reflex Angle: An angle that's bigger than 180°! For example, 225° is a reflex angle. Reflex angles sort of look like they're "on the outside" instead of "between" our two arms . . . but you're not likely to have to work with them quite yet.

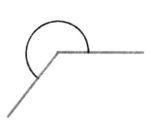

Protractors

Get ready to meet . . . drumroll please . . . THE PROTRACTOR! So, you know how we use rulers to measure the length of lines? Well, protractors are our super-secret weapons for measuring the size of angles!

There are many types of protractor, but the most common ones look like this . . .

The Semicircular!

WITH a hole in the middle
(just like a doughnut) . . .

VERY POPULAR!

. . . and without one!

The Circular!

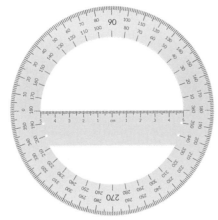

It's all-round fun!

The Triangular!

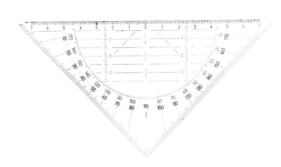

But how did it get its name?
(I'm TRI-ng to figure it out!)

PROTRACTOR BASICS

It's time to get to know our new pal, the protractor! Most elementary classrooms use semicircular protractors. They're perfect for measuring angles up to 180°, and that's all you really need to do at this point. So, let's start measuring angles!

Your protractor is divided up into 180°, so there are 180 tiny subdivisions (like, those little tick marks) around the outside.

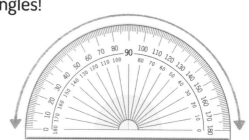

You can measure both **acute angles**, like these:

Acute angles are LESS than 90°. Aren't they cute?

. . . And **obtuse angles**, like these:

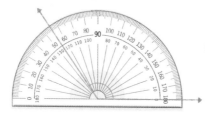

Obtuse angles are GREATER than 90°.

☆ MEMORIZE THIS!

Acute sounds like "a cute" angle, so think of a cute little bunny — which is SMALLer than 90° — a CUTE angle. Obtuse rhymes with "moose" — and moose are BIGger than 90° — a super-large angle!

70

Oh, and let's not forget **right angles** . . .   . . . Or **straight angles**!

Right angles are
EXACTLY 90°.

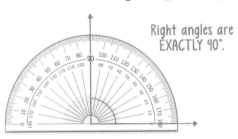

Straight angles
are always 180°.

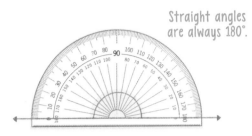

PROTRACTORS: UP CLOSE AND PERSONAL

On the outside scale,
the numbers increase
from LEFT to RIGHT, or
CLOCKWISE, starting
at zero.

On the inside scale
the numbers increase
from RIGHT to LEFT, or
COUNTER-CLOCKWISE,
starting at zero.

This is zero on the
outside scale.

This is also zero, but
for the inside scale.

Each tiny
mark
represents 1°.

WATCH OUT!

The biggest mistake kids make when using
a protractor is using the wrong set of
numbers! Notice that there are two sets
of measurements: one that runs along the
top and another set underneath. The set of
numbers you use matters.

USING A PROTRACTOR TO MEASURE ANGLES UP TO 180°

I'm going to show you what it's like to measure an acute AND an obtuse angle so you can get the hang of measuring both! Just follow the steps, and you'll be an angle-measuring PRO in no time!

Q: What size is this acute angle?

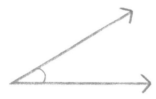

> * Make sure you pick the right number! If the angle is acute, use the smaller number. If the angle is obtuse, use the bigger number.

Step 1: Find the middle dot on the bottom line of your protractor, and place it on the vertex of the angle.

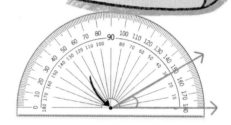

Step 2: Make sure the 0° mark is lined up perfectly with the arm.

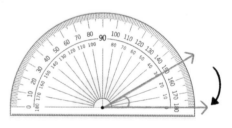

Step 3: Now, the moment of truth: look on your scale to see what number the OTHER arm lines up with! What number is it pointing to? Remember, this angle is acute, which means it HAS to be SMALLER than 90°! (Hint: it's not gonna be that 150° number.)

A: This acute angle is 30°.

ARROWS OR NO ARROWS? Some teachers like to use 'em on the end of a line, some don't. Sometimes you see them in your workbook, sometimes you don't. Best thing to do: check with your teacher for how they'd like you to do it. It's all good.

Q: What size is this obtuse angle?

Step 1: Find the middle dot on the bottom line of your protractor, and place it on the vertex of the angle.

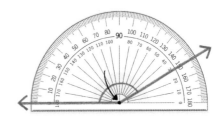

Step 2: Make sure the 0° mark of your protractor is perfectly lined up with the arm of the angle.

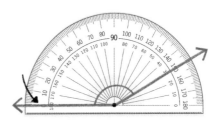

Step 3: Now, the fun part! Look on your scale to see what number the other arm lines up with! What number is it pointing to? Remember, this angle is obtuse, which means that it HAS to be BIGGER than 90°!

A: This obtuse angle is 150°.

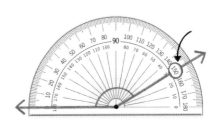

JUST FYI!

In **step 2**, if you lined up the OTHER arm of your obtuse angle to the bottom, you would still get 150°. Move your protractor (or the page, whatever is easier!) so it lines up on the other arm. Check it out:

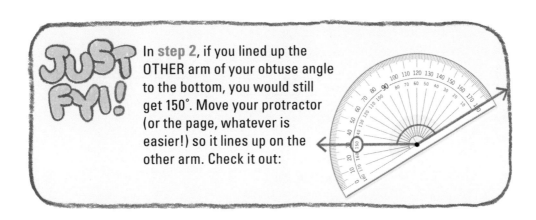

USING A PROTRACTOR TO DRAW ANGLES UP TO 180°

Okay, now we're going to learn how to draw an angle with a protractor. Grab a protractor, pencil, eraser and ruler — let's get to it!

Q: How do we draw a 60° angle?

Step 1: Use a ruler (or the flat side of your protractor) to draw a straight line. Mark a point on it, somewhere near the middle if possible! This will become the first arm of your angle.

Step 2: Put your protractor's centre on that point. Now, you're going upward from the zero, along the scale that increases from right to left. Read the numbers from right to left until you get to 60°! Follow the line up to where you can mark a little dot on your paper.

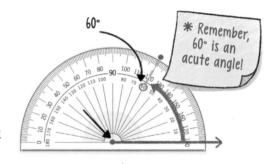

60°

* Remember, 60° is an acute angle!

Step 3: Using a ruler, draw a line between the points you marked in the first and second steps. Remember, those points are the vertex and the dot at 60°. Voila! You have the second arm of your angle.

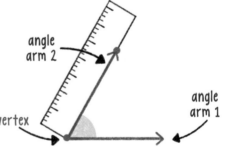

angle arm 2

angle arm 1

vertex

Step 4: Colour in your angle and label it for extra marks. You are DONE!

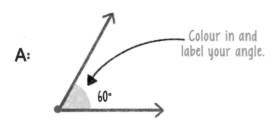

A:

Colour in and label your angle.

60°

Q: Let's draw a 120° angle.

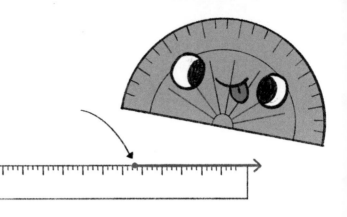

Step 1: Again, use the flat edge of your protractor (or a ruler) to draw a straight line. Mark a point on it — near the middle works best! This will become the first arm of your angle.

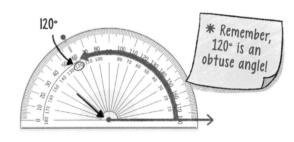

Step 2: Put your protractor's centre on that point. Now, you're going upward from the zero, along the scale that increases from right to left. Read the numbers from right to left until you get to 120°! Follow the line up to where you can mark a little dot on your paper.

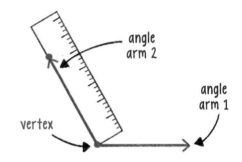

120°

* Remember, 120° is an obtuse angle!

Step 3: Using the edge of your protractor (or a ruler), draw a line between the points you marked in the first and second steps. Remember, those points are the vertex and the dot at 120°. Ta-da! You have the second arm of your angle.

angle arm 2

angle arm 1

vertex

Step 4: Colour in your angle, then label it with that bright, shiny 120°, and you are DONE!

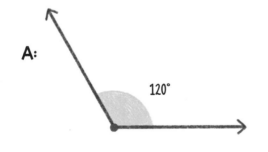

A:

120°

You NEED to use a ruler (or the flat side of your protractor) to draw a straight line, and you NEED to use a protractor to draw an angle perfectly. Use the tools or you will TOTALLY lose marks.

TWO-DIMENSIONAL SHAPES

Flat's All, Folks!

What even are they?! **Two-dimensional shapes** are flat, just like shapes we draw on paper. We say they have two dimensions because they have length and width . . . but no thickness. So they're missing that third dimension. Heads-up: if you see the term "2-D," that's just a quick 'n' cool way to say two-dimensional.

These are ALL 2-D shapes. Two-dimensional shapes can have straight or curvy edges, or even both!

Fancy Lingo!

If you want to sound super smart, another name for a 2-D shape is a **plane figure**. Here, plane means something that is flat — not the thing that flies in the sky.

SHAPES ARE FUN!
What did the rectangle say to the circle?

Hey, I haven't seen you around!

POLYGONS VS. NON-POLYGONS

What does that mean? This is where shapes get exciting! Any closed 2-D shape whose sides are all straight line segments is called a **polygon**. And there are all different kinds of polygons! To figure out what kind of polygon you've got, you need to look at:

1. The number of sides it has
2. The angles formed by its sides

What the heck is an angle?! Don't worry, I've got you covered! Head to page 64 to learn all about angles!

Team Polygon

Team Non-Polygon

This cloud is a closed shape, but its sides aren't straight!

Team Not a Shape at All!

This zigzag is made of line segments, but it isn't a closed shape, so it's NOT a polygon!

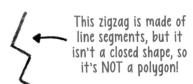

Fancy Lingo!

When a shape's side lengths and angles are ALL the EXACT SAME as another shape's, we say those two shapes are **congruent**. Congruent shapes are like identical twins.

77

POLYGON PARTS

Before we start giving polygons names, we need to learn how we even talk about them. Here are some of the words and symbols we use to describe polygons!

Vertices: Each corner of a polygon where two sides meet is called a **vertex**. When we're talking about more than one vertex, we refer to them as **vertices**. So, this wacky shape has four vertices!

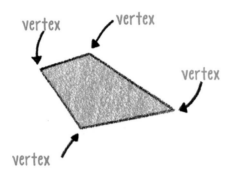

Sides: A line segment joining any two vertices of a shape is called a **side**. We can show that certain sides are the same length by marking them with dashes. Any sides that have the same number of dashes are the same length! We can also show that certain sides are parallel by marking them with little arrows. Sides with the same number of arrows are parallel to one another.

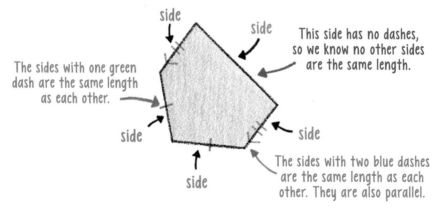

Interior Angles: When we're talking about shapes, we're really interested in the angles formed by sides that are next to one another, like, on the inside of the figure. We call these **interior angles**. The cool thing is that we can show certain angles are the exact same size by using different symbols or colours. Angles with the same symbol or colour are the same!

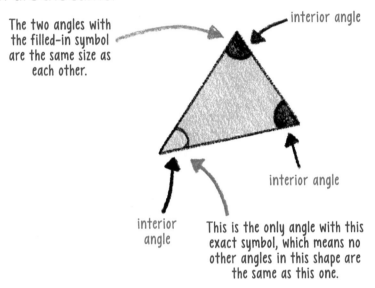

The two angles with the filled-in symbol are the same size as each other.

interior angle

interior angle

interior angle

This is the only angle with this exact symbol, which means no other angles in this shape are the same as this one.

Diagonals: A **diagonal** is a line segment joining two vertices that aren't right next to each other! Diagonals can be inside or outside of a shape, but we mostly talk about the inside ones!

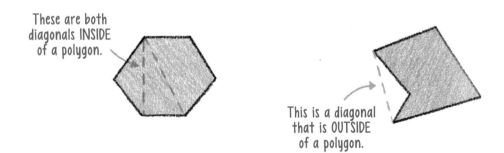

These are both diagonals INSIDE of a polygon.

This is a diagonal that is OUTSIDE of a polygon.

REGULAR AND IRREGULAR POLYGONS

Polygons can be split into two basic categories: A **regular polygon**, where all sides are the same length and all angles are the same size, and an **irregular polygon**, where the sides and angles aren't all the same. The same family of shapes can contain both regular and irregular polygons. Check out these triangles, for example:

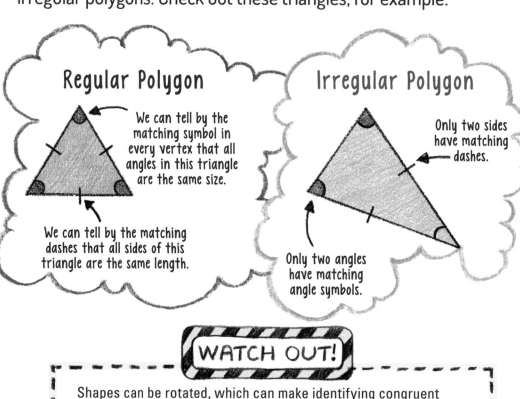

Regular Polygon

We can tell by the matching symbol in every vertex that all angles in this triangle are the same size.

We can tell by the matching dashes that all sides of this triangle are the same length.

Irregular Polygon

Only two sides have matching dashes.

Only two angles have matching angle symbols.

WATCH OUT!

Shapes can be rotated, which can make identifying congruent shapes very tricky. Remember, their "personality traits" are the only thing that matters. Pay close attention to their side lengths and angles. Inspect them closely! Even if the two shapes are oriented differently, you might find that by rotating or flipping them, they turn out to be congruent, and identical twins after all.

Meet the Famous Polygons!

There are lots and lots of polygons out there, but here are the ones you NEED to know. The most common polygons are triangles and quadrilaterals, so let's start there.

TRIANGLES

A triangle has three sides, three angles and three vertices. There are different types of triangles in the triangle family, but all of them share these qualities. We sort the different types of triangles based on two things:

1. The lengths of their sides
2. The sizes of their angles

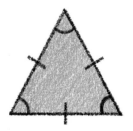

Fancy Lingo!

"**Tri**" means "three" in Greek.

TRIANGLES — GET TO KNOW THEM!

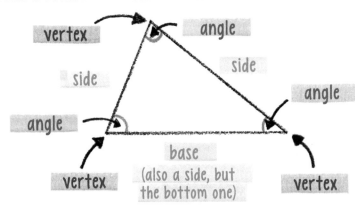

vertex

angle

side

side

angle

angle

vertex

base
(also a side, but
the bottom one)

vertex

Equilateral Triangles

Length of sides: All three sides are the exact same length

Size of angles: All three angles are the exact same measure or size

Isosceles Triangles

Length of sides: Only two sides are the exact same length

Size of angles: The two angles opposite the equal sides are the same measure or size

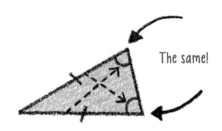

The same!

Scalene Triangles

Length of sides: None of the sides are the same length

Size of angles: None of the angles are the same measure or size

Since no sides have dashes and no angles have matching symbols, we can tell that all sides and all angles are different.

Right Triangles

Length of sides: Either two sides are the same length or none of the sides are the same length

Size of angles: One angle is always a right angle, which equals 90°, and the other two angles might be the same as one another, or they might be different, but they are always acute

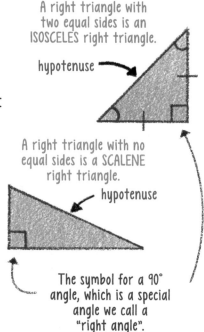

A right triangle with two equal sides is an ISOSCELES right triangle.

hypotenuse

A right triangle with no equal sides is a SCALENE right triangle.

hypotenuse

The symbol for a 90° angle, which is a special angle we call a "right angle".

FUN Fact!

The longest side of a right triangle is always across from the 90 degree angle. This side is called the hypotenuse.

QUADRILATERALS

A quadrilateral is a special type of polygon that has four sides, four angles and four vertices. There are different types of quadrilaterals in our quad family, but all of them share these qualities! We name different types of quadrilaterals depending on three things:

1. The lengths of their sides
2. The direction of their sides
3. The sizes of their angles

> **Fancy Lingo!**
> "**Quad**" means "four" in Latin!

There are many different quadrilaterals, but I'm just going to show you the most common ones. It might help you to flip back to pages 56 and 57 for a refresher on **parallel** and **perpendicular** first!

Rectangles

Length of sides: The sides opposite one another are the exact same length

Direction of sides: The sides opposite one another are parallel, and the sides next to each other are perpendicular

Size of angles: All four angles are right angles

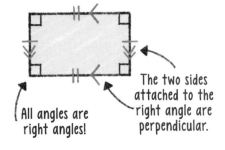

All angles are right angles!

The two sides attached to the right angle are perpendicular.

Squares

Length of sides: All sides are exactly the same length

Direction of sides: The sides opposite one another are parallel and the sides next to each other are perpendicular

Size of angles: All four angles are right angles

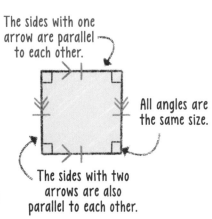

The sides with one arrow are parallel to each other.

All angles are the same size.

The sides with two arrows are also parallel to each other.

Parallelograms

Length of sides: The sides opposite one another are the exact same length

Direction of sides: There are two pairs of parallel sides that are opposite each other

Size of angles: Angles opposite each other are equal

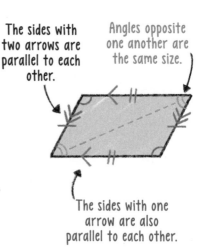

The sides with two arrows are parallel to each other.

Angles opposite one another are the same size.

The sides with one arrow are also parallel to each other.

Rhombuses

Length of sides: All sides are the exact same length

Direction of sides: The sides opposite one another are parallel

Size of angles: Angles opposite each other are equal

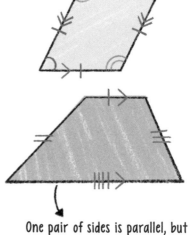

A rhombus is a special kind of parallelogram, where ALL of its sides are the exact same length.

Trapezoids

Length of sides: Each side is a totally different length

Direction of sides: Only one pair of sides is parallel

Size of angles: It can vary — sometimes they have two the same, sometimes none the same

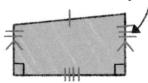

One pair of sides is parallel, but no sides are the same length.

COOL Fact!

Squares are technically a kind of parallelogram AND a kind of rhombus! Squares follow the same rules as these shapes — but squares always have four right angles.

Isosceles Trapezoids

Length of sides: One pair of opposite sides is the same length — this is different than a regular trapezoid!

Direction of sides: Only one pair of sides is parallel and these two sides do NOT have the same length

Size of angles: Both angles attached to one parallel side are equal, and both angles attached to the other parallel side are also equal

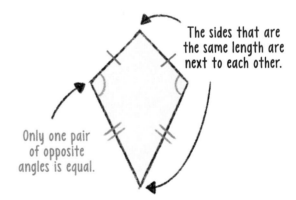

Opposite sides (with two lines) are the same length but NOT parallel.

Angles attached to one parallel side are the same size as each other.

Angles attached to the other parallel side are the same size as each other.

Kites

Length of sides: Two pairs of same-length sides — the sides that are the same length are always next to each other

Direction of sides: None of the sides are parallel

Size of angles: One pair of opposite angles is equal, and the other two angles are different

The sides that are the same length are next to each other.

Only one pair of opposite angles is equal.

Fancy Lingo!
We use the word **"adjacent"** to describe things that are next to, or beside, each other. In a kite, adjacent sides have the same length.

QUADRILATERAL TIP SHEET!

Some of these shapes share the same rules. In the quadrilateral family, many shapes can be called more than one thing.

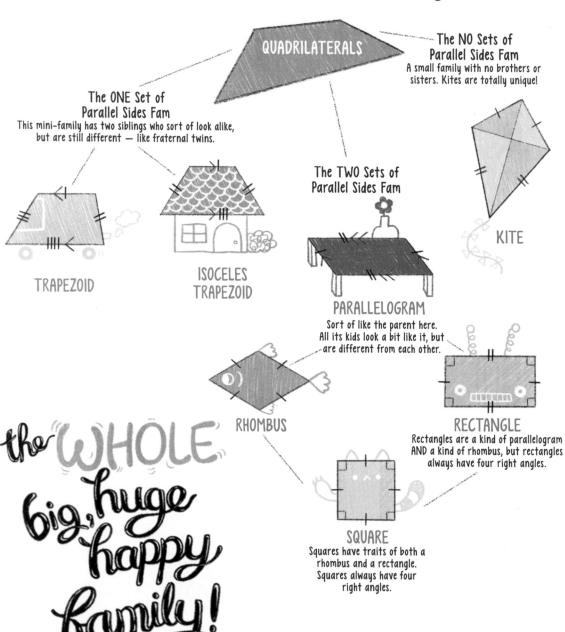

QUADRILATERALS

The NO Sets of Parallel Sides Fam
A small family with no brothers or sisters. Kites are totally unique!

The ONE Set of Parallel Sides Fam
This mini-family has two siblings who sort of look alike, but are still different — like fraternal twins.

The TWO Sets of Parallel Sides Fam

KITE

TRAPEZOID

ISOCELES TRAPEZOID

PARALLELOGRAM
Sort of like the parent here. All its kids look a bit like it, but are different from each other.

RHOMBUS

RECTANGLE
Rectangles are a kind of parallelogram AND a kind of rhombus, but rectangles always have four right angles.

SQUARE
Squares have traits of both a rhombus and a rectangle. Squares always have four right angles.

the WHOLE big, huge happy family!

86

WHAT ABOUT OTHER POLYGONS?!

Triangles and quadrilaterals are cool, but there are SO many other polygons out there — and there's a trick to knowing what they are called. For starters, a polygon always has the same number of sides as it has angles. The trick for those other polygons is knowing the Latin or Greek word for the number of angles tacked on to the front of "gon." And what does "gon" mean? Basically a "shape with a number of angles." If you know the magic word for that number, you can name that polygon!

Magic Word Hack	It means the number...	POLYGON NAME	Looks Kinda like...	
			REGULAR POLYGON	IRREGULAR POLYGON
TRI	3	Triangle		
QUAD	4	Quadrilateral		
PENTA	5	Pentagon		
HEXA	6	Hexagon		

REGULAR POLYGON   IRREGULAR POLYGON

HEPTA	7	Heptagon		
OCTA	8	Octagon		
NONA	9	Nonagon		
DECA	10	Decagon		
HENDECA	11	Hendacagon		
DODECA	12	Dodecagon		

FUN Fact!

You'll probably NEVER use "hendeca" in your actual math class.

THREE-DIMENSIONAL SHAPES

Top Secrets Revealed!

What even are they?! A **three-dimensional shape** is anything that has length, width and thickness. Shapes can be hollow or solid. For example, an empty shoebox is a 3-D shape, and so is a brick.

These are ALL 3-D shapes! Literally anything in the real world that's not drawn on a piece of paper or on a computer screen is a 3-D shape — anything at all!

Even a piece of paper is a 3-D shape — though it is super thin, it still has some thickness.

thickness or height

length

width

When you see "3-D" written, it's just short for three-dimensional. Writing it as 3-D is cooler and quicker.

WHAT MAKES A 3-D SHAPE WHAT IT IS?

Many 3-D shapes have **faces**, **edges** and **vertices**. Let's have a look!

Faces

Many 3-D shapes have surfaces made up of 2-D shapes. We call these surfaces **faces**. You can think of faces as flat — both words start with an F! There is one special face called the **base**. It's the one that is perpendicular (see page 57) to the direction we'd measure height. It's often the face that your shape SITS on — like, the one at the bottom — and in many cases the one that gives your shape its name. A sphere, on the other hand, doesn't have ANY faces at all!

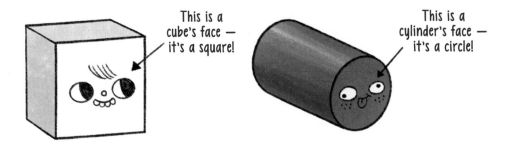

This is a cube's face — it's a square!

This is a cylinder's face — it's a circle!

Edges

Picture tracing ONE of your shape's faces. What you are tracing are the face's edges. An edge is where two faces meet.

There are four edges on this cube's face!

There is one edge on this cylinder's face!

Vertices

A **vertex** is the pointy part of a 3-D shape where three (or more!) edges meet. The word "vertices" is the plural of vertex. If your shape has a pointy part right at the top, and it is the point farthest away from the base, that vertex has a special name. We call it an **apex**.

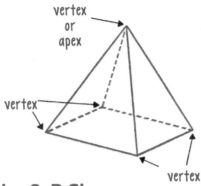

The Most Popular 3-D Shapes

There are bajillions of 3-D shapes out there, from your shoe to the planet Jupiter. But there are certain ones you NEED to know for math class. When we want to figure out what to call a 3-D shape, we look at these four major things:

1. Their bases
2. Their faces
3. Their edges
4. Their vertices

I know when I was talking about 2-D shapes, I said **vertex** was used to describe the spot where two sides met. That's true for 2-D shapes, but when we talk about 3-D shapes, it means something different! Just like in the real world, in math sometimes words have different meanings depending on what you're talking about!

SPHERES

A sphere is an object that is completely round and shaped like a ball. It has one smooth surface around the entire shape. Think of a basketball or a gumball.

Bases: Nope, no bases

Faces: It doesn't have any!

Edges: None of these either

Vertices: And zero of these as well

SECRET POWER!

Any point you touch on a sphere's surface is the same distance from its centre as all the other points on its surface.

Fancy Lingo!

Pssst: Want to know a super-fancy word for all of that? **Equidistant!** Because equi (equal) + distant = equidistant. All points on a sphere's surface are equidistant from its centre!

PRISMS

All prisms have something in common: the sides are always parallelograms. The base has a twin, another face on the other end that is identical and parallel. The shape of the base tells you what kind of prism you have. Let's look at a couple!

REMEMBER?!

A square is a kind of rectangle . . . and a rectangle is a kind of parallelogram!

Rectangular Prisms

A rectangular prism looks like a box. Think of a juice box or a brick. These are sometimes called **cuboid**.

Bases: Its bases are rectangles

Faces: It has six faces and they're all rectangles

Edges: It has twelve edges

Vertices: It has eight vertices

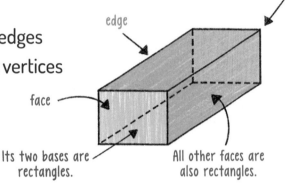

vertex

edge

face

Its two bases are rectangles.

All other faces are also rectangles.

Cubes

A cube is a super-special type of rectangular prism whose faces are all the EXACT SAME SIZE.

Bases: Its bases are squares

Faces: It has six identical faces

Edges: It has twelve edges

Vertices: It has eight vertices

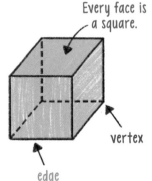

Every face is a square.

vertex

edge

A cube has the same number of bases, edges and vertices as a rectangular prism, BUT what makes them different is that its edges are ALL the same length and its faces are ALL squares of the same size!

Plenty of Prisms!

There are countless other prisms out there. To figure out what kind you've got, it's all about the base! That base can be ANY polygon — rectangle, triangle, pentagon, you name it!

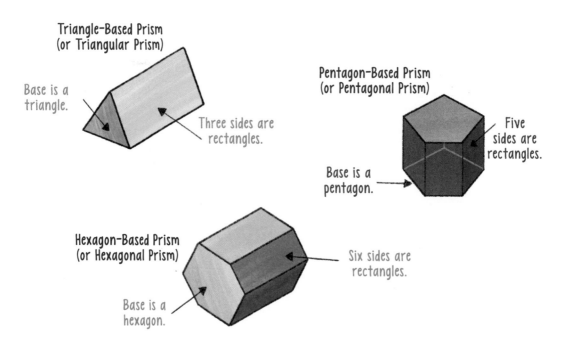

Triangle-Based Prism (or Triangular Prism)

Base is a triangle.

Three sides are rectangles.

Pentagon-Based Prism (or Pentagonal Prism)

Five sides are rectangles.

Base is a pentagon.

Hexagon-Based Prism (or Hexagonal Prism)

Six sides are rectangles.

Base is a hexagon.

Ready to level up?

Meet this guy, the oblique prism! An oblique prism can come in any of the prism shapes, only this time the bases are NOT on top of each other. The sides are parallelograms, but they are NOT all rectangles.

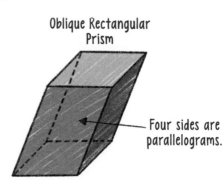

Oblique Rectangular Prism

Four sides are parallelograms.

CYLINDERS

A cylinder has two circular bases joined together by a curved surface — like a soup can. If you removed the label from that can, you'd see that the curved surface is a rectangle in disguise!

SECRET POWER!
The circle at the top is identical to the one at the bottom.

Bases: Its bases are circles

Faces: It has two faces — they are bases, with one curved rectangle between them

Edges: It has two edges —one around each base

Vertices: None

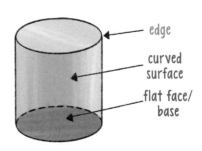

CONES

A cone has a circular base and a curved surface. Think of a party hat! If you flattened the curved face, you'd have part of a circle.

Bases: Its base is a circle

Faces: It has one face, which is also the base

Edges: It has one edge, around the base

Vertices: One apex/vertex at the top

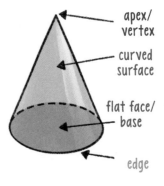

Ready to level up?

Just like the oblique rectangular prism, there can be oblique cylinders and oblique cones!

Oblique Cylinder   Oblique Cone

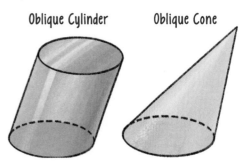

PYRAMIDS

Like prisms, there are all kinds of different pyramids. But all pyramids have something in common: every single face that is NOT the base is a triangle, and ALL of those triangles have to meet at a point, or vertex. The base can be ANY polygon! Like, a triangle, a square, or even an octagon! But we don't know how many faces, edges and vertices a pyramid has UNLESS we know its base. The most common are triangle-, rectangle-, and square-based pyramids, so let's have a look!

Triangle-Based Pyramids

Also known as a triangular pyramid.

Bases: Its base is a triangle

Faces: It has four faces, all triangles

Edges: It has six edges

Vertices: It has four vertices, including the apex

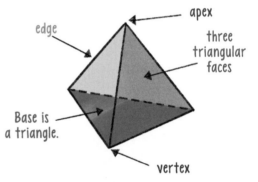

A triangular prism is very different from a triangular pyramid.

Rectangle-Based Pyramids

Also known as a rectangular pyramid.

Bases: Its base is a rectangle

Faces: It has five faces — four triangles and one rectangle

Edges: It has eight edges

Vertices: It has five vertices, including the apex

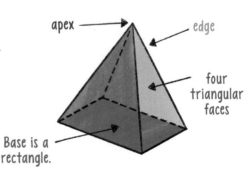

Square-Based Pyramids

Also known as a square pyramid.

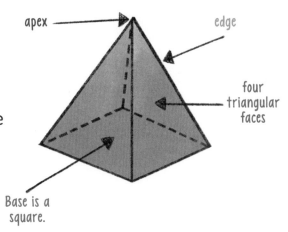

apex

edge

four
triangular
faces

Base is a
square.

Bases: Its base is a square

Faces: It has five faces:
four triangles and one square

Edges: It has eight edges

Vertices: It has five vertices,
including the apex

Polyhedrons

Poly-WHATrons?! I know — it sounds like we're about to talk about something super complicated. But it's not hard, promise!

A **polyhedron** is a three-dimensional shape made up of polygons. It has flat faces. So, prisms and pyramids are polyhedrons, but cones, cylinders and spheres are not. But the story doesn't end there!

Fancy Lingo!

The word "poly" means many. And if you guessed that "hedron" basically means face, you'd be right. That's why these guys are called **polyhedrons** — because they have MANY faces.

Regular Polyhedrons

It may not sound like a **regular polyhedron** is special — but it totally is. All of its faces are the EXACT same regular polygon. A cube is a regular polyhedron because every single face is the same square. There are only five regular **polyhedrons** IN THE WORLD, so get excited to meet them!

How do we figure out which regular polyhedron is which? You really only need to look at the NUMBER of faces.

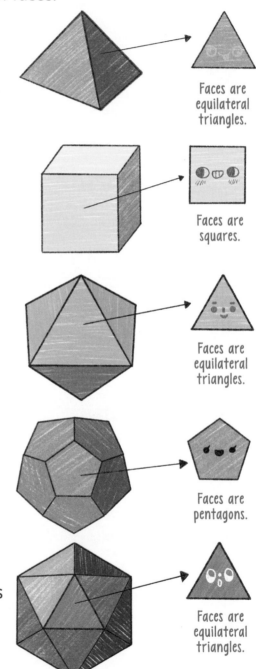

Tetrahedrons

Faces: Four equilateral triangles
Edges: Six
Vertices: Four

Faces are equilateral triangles.

Cubes

Faces: Six squares
Edges: Twelve
Vertices: Eight

Faces are squares.

Octahedrons

Faces: Eight equilateral triangles
Edges: Twelve
Vertices: Six

Faces are equilateral triangles.

Dodecahedrons

Faces: Twelve regular pentagons
Edges: Thirty
Vertices: Twenty

Faces are pentagons.

Icosahedrons

Faces: Twenty equilateral triangles
Edges: Thirty
Vertices: Twelve

Faces are equilateral triangles.

SYMMETRY

Mirror, Mirror on the Wall

What even is it?! **Symmetry** is when a shape has parts that exactly match each other after a flip or turn. There are different kinds of symmetry — we'll take a look at **reflective** and **rotational**.

REFLECTIVE SYMMETRY

Reflective symmetry means that you can divide a shape EXACTLY in half. Imagine folding a square of paper in half. Now, unfold that square of paper and you have a line straight down the middle. That line divides your page in half, and both sides are the same.

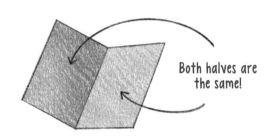

Both halves are the same!

If you can draw a line through the middle of a shape, and there are two identical halves that fit exactly onto each other, then your shape is symmetrical! We also call reflective symmetry **mirror symmetry**. If you stick a mirror in the middle of your shape, the shape plus the reflection would look like the WHOLE shape — the same on both sides.

If you put a mirror next to this half-butterfly shape . . .

mirror line

. . . the reflection makes a picture of a whole butterfly!

reflection

SYMMETRY VS. ASYMMETRY

If a shape has symmetry, we call it **symmetrical**. If it doesn't have symmetry, we stick an "a" in front of it and call it **asymmetrical**. The prefix "a" means "not" or "without."

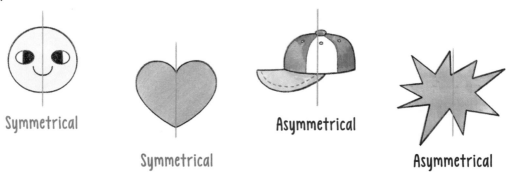

Symmetrical

Symmetrical

Asymmetrical

Asymmetrical

LINES OF SYMMETRY

When we're talking about reflective symmetry, the line that divides a shape in half to give us two matching half-shapes is called a **line** or **axis of symmetry**, or a **mirror line**. (It doesn't have to be a REAL line. It can be an imaginary line!) There can be horizontal, vertical and slant lines of symmetry. Some shapes have multiple lines of symmetry! To figure out how many lines of symmetry a shape has, we just draw 'em in and count 'em!

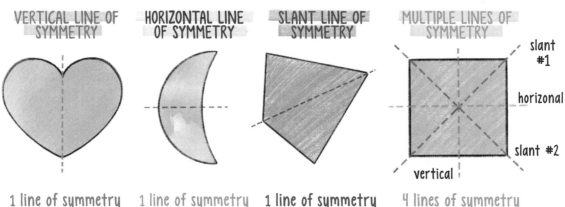

VERTICAL LINE OF SYMMETRY

HORIZONTAL LINE OF SYMMETRY

SLANT LINE OF SYMMETRY

MULTIPLE LINES OF SYMMETRY

slant #1

horizonal

slant #2

vertical

1 line of symmetry   1 line of symmetry   1 line of symmetry   4 lines of symmetry

ROTATIONAL SYMMETRY

Rotational symmetry is when we can turn a shape around on a point in the middle so that the shape fits exactly onto itself. Imagine a snowflake with a pin in the middle — if we spin it a certain amount, it will sit exactly on top of its original outline. That's it!

Centre of Rotational Symmetry

The point a shape spins around is called its **centre of rotational symmetry**. There is only one, always hanging out there in the middle. Check out this snowflake. Its centre of rotational symmetry is that point in the centre marked with a dot.

You can rotate a shape around ANY point you want — think of sticking a pin somewhere else on this page and turning the snowflake around that. But that's a TOTALLY different thing than the centre of rotational symmetry.

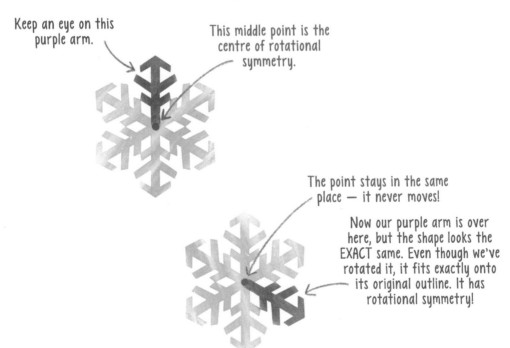

Keep an eye on this purple arm.

This middle point is the centre of rotational symmetry.

The point stays in the same place — it never moves!

Now our purple arm is over here, but the shape looks the EXACT same. Even though we've rotated it, it fits exactly onto its original outline. It has rotational symmetry!

ORDER OF ROTATIONAL SYMMETRY

Okay, so imagine you've stuck a pin in the middle of your shape. How many times does your shape fit onto its original outline in one full 360° turn? That number is called the **order of rotational symmetry**. To see that, watch the star's purple point as it rotates clockwise. It can fit right on top of its original outline five times. That means it has a rotational symmetry of five.

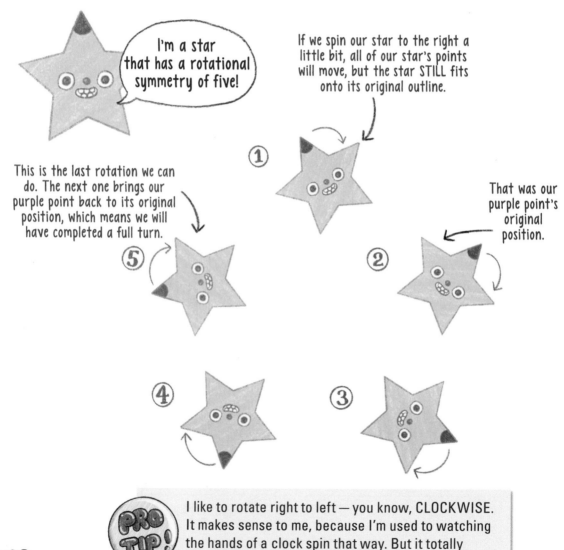

I'm a star that has a rotational symmetry of five!

If we spin our star to the right a little bit, all of our star's points will move, but the star STILL fits onto its original outline.

①

That was our purple point's original position.

This is the last rotation we can do. The next one brings our purple point back to its original position, which means we will have completed a full turn.

⑤ ② ④ ③

PRO TIP! I like to rotate right to left — you know, CLOCKWISE. It makes sense to me, because I'm used to watching the hands of a clock spin that way. But it totally works the other way too.

REFLECTIVE AND ROTATIONAL SYMMETRY TIPSHEET

By playing around with different shapes, you can easily figure out how many lines of symmetry they have, as well as their order of rotational symmetry. Here's a quick tipsheet to help with some common shapes.

EQUILATERAL TRIANGLES

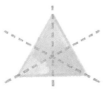

Lines of symmetry: 3
Order of rotational symmetry: 3

RECTANGLES

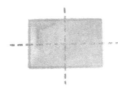

Lines of symmetry: 2
Order of rotational symmetry: 2

REGULAR PENTAGONS

Lines of symmetry: 5
Order of rotational symmetry: 5

REGULAR HEPTAGONS

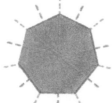

Lines of symmetry: 7
Order of rotational symmetry: 7

SQUARES

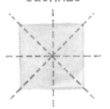

Lines of symmetry: 4
Order of rotational symmetry: 4

RHOMBUSES

Lines of symmetry: 2
Order of rotational symmetry: 2

REGULAR HEXAGONS

Lines of symmetry: 6
Order of rotational symmetry: 6

REGULAR OCTAGONS

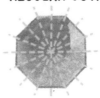

Lines of symmetry: 8
Order of rotational symmetry: 8

ONE ORDER OF ROTATIONAL SYMMETRY

For these shapes, you'd have to turn them ALL the way around back to where you started for them to fit back into themselves. So, that's an order of rotational symmetry of — you guessed it! — one.

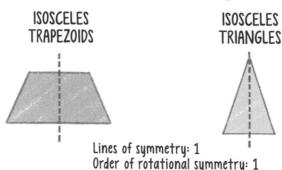

ISOSCELES
TRAPEZOIDS

ISOSCELES
TRIANGLES

Lines of symmetry: 1
Order of rotational symmetry: 1

PARALLELOGRAMS

TRAPEZOIDS

SCALENE
TRIANGLES

Lines of symmetry: ZERO!
Order of rotational symmetry: 1

what?

If a rhombus has two lines of symmetry and an order of rotational symmetry of two, and it's a parallelogram, then why doesn't any old parallelogram? The secret power of a rhombus is its sides. They're all equal in length — and that's the key. Look at this parallelogram. See? If you check out the shapes on either side of the reflecting line, they are NOT the mirror image of each other.

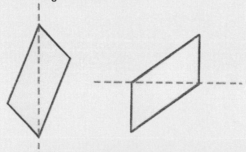

SUPERSTAR CIRCLES

Circles are the ONLY shapes that have infinite lines of symmetry and an infinite order of rotational symmetry! What does that even mean? It means there are ENDLESS lines of symmetry you could draw and ENDLESS ways you could rotate it so it would still cover itself up.

Lines of symmetry: infinite!
Order of rotational symmetry: also infinite!

Fancy Lingo!

Infinite comes from the Latin word "infinitus," which means "without end." Infinite usually means that something goes on forever and ever and ever . . .

TRANSFORMATIONS
Making Shapes Dance

What even are they?! You got your shape . . . now move it around! Shapes dancing — that's legit all a **transformation** is. We'll look at three major types of transformation here: **reflections**, **translations** and **rotations**.

REFLECTIONS

Reflections basically flip a shape over an imaginary line, like a mirror. We call the shape that you start with the **object** and the shape you get

Fancy Lingo!

These transformations make **congruent** shapes. Shapes are congruent if they're the EXACT same shape and size as each other. All the sides are the same length, and all angles are the same size. Imagine cutting a shape out. If you can turn, flip or move it to fit EXACTLY on top of another one, they're congruent shapes.

when you flip it the **image** — because it's like a mirror image! The magic line the object is flipped over is called the **mirror line** OR the **reflection line**!

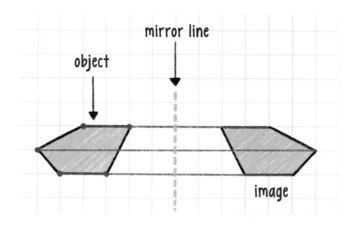

How do we reflect an object?

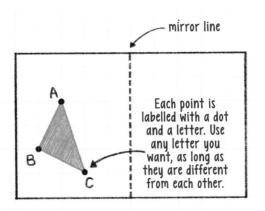

mirror line

Each point is labelled with a dot and a letter. Use any letter you want, as long as they are different from each other.

Step 1: Draw your object on GRAPH PAPER. I chose a triangle, because I felt like it, but you can try this with a rectangle or rhombus or whatever! Then, mark each important point with a dot. Important points are usually corners, or vertices, of your shape. Label them with different letters — it will help you keep track of what's going on as you move each one.

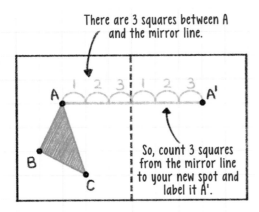

There are 3 squares between A and the mirror line.

So, count 3 squares from the mirror line to your new spot and label it A'.

Step 2: Start with point A. Moving horizontally along the grid line, count the number of squares until you hit the mirror line. That's your magic number for that point! Here, it's 3. Use that SAME number to count the squares on the other side of your mirror line. Label that point A' (you read this as "A prime"). Think of it as, "This is A in the universe on this side of the mirror."

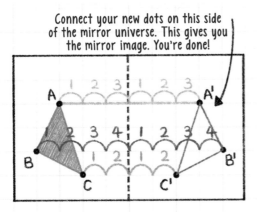

Connect your new dots on this side of the mirror universe. This gives you the mirror image. You're done!

Step 3: Repeat step 2 for all of the other points you have. Here, you have B and C. Connect the points, and you're done! You have a mirror image of your triangle. YAY!

TRANSLATIONS

Translations might just be the easiest transformation! All we're doing is sliding our shape into a new position by moving it up or down, and left or right. Let's use our friendly graph paper and a quadrilateral with labelled vertices to see what that looks like.

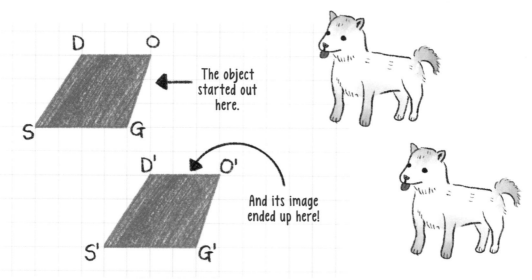

The object started out here.

And its image ended up here!

How do we translate an object?

You can translate a shape by counting or by using the coordinate grid. If you need a refresher on coordinates, flip back to page 45. Either way you go, ALWAYS USE GRAPH PAPER for your translations. Don't even try these not on a grid!

REPEAT THIS RHYME EVERY TIME!

A great way to avoid mistakes?
Label EVERY corner of your shapes!

Translating objects by counting

Let's translate this friendly little triangle 2 units right and 3 units up.

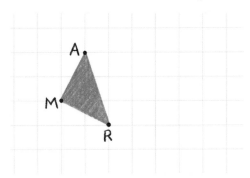

Step 1: Make sure your triangle is drawn neatly, with the vertices (corner points!) labelled. Put little dots on those points so you can track them in the next step.

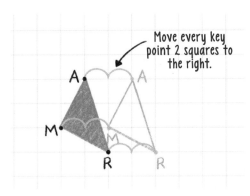

Move every key point 2 squares to the right.

Step 2: Do one translation — or move — at a time. First, move ALL of your key points 2 squares to the right! You can connect them with lines so that you can SEE your shape — it's the exact same shape, just moved over. (P.S. You can do your translations in EITHER order. So, you could move all the points up 3 units and THEN right 2 units.)

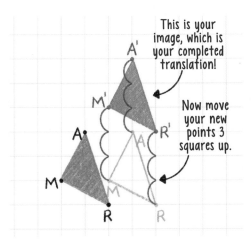

This is your image, which is your completed translation!

Now move your new points 3 squares up.

Step 3: Next, take those new points from step 2 and move them all 3 squares up. Connect the three new dots (WITH A RULER), label the points A', R' and M' and you are DONE! That's your friendly triangle, translated 2 units to the right and 3 units up.

Bonus points: Now, head back to the quadrilateral labelled DOGS. Can you use this counting hack to figure out how it's been translated? (Answer below)

A: If you got 3 units to the right and 5 units down, you got it right!

109

Translating objects using the coordinate system

If you need to translate a shape using the coordinate system, you got this! All you have to do is count steps along the x and y axes. Normally, I like doing translations in two steps (left or right and up or down) to make sure I don't make a mistake. But if you want to show off your math skills, you can do it in one step. And that's what I'll show you here!

Q: What are the new coordinates of the image CAT after the following translation: $(x, y) \rightarrow (x + 4, y + 3)$?

Try it: To find the answer, you need move EVERY point 4 units right and then 3 units up. Or if you feel like it, 3 up and then 4 right! After you do that, you can note the new coordinates of the points.

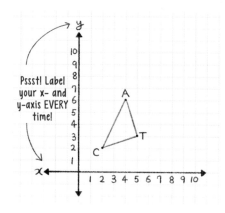

Pssst! Label your x- and y-axis EVERY time!

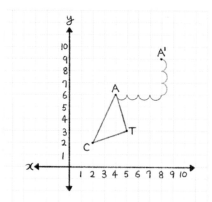

Step 1: Deal with one point at a time. Move "A" 4 units to the right and 3 units up. Simple! Remember to stick the tick mark (') next to your new point, so A becomes A'. Repeat that for the other points. Label them so you don't get mixed up!

JUST FYI! We made these grids way smaller so they fit better on the page. But when you do them, use normal-size graph paper!

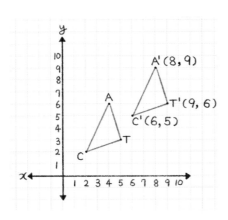

Step 2: See where you are for each new point along the x-axis and y-axis and record them. Remember, coordinates go in alphabetical order: (x, y).

A: Our new points are:
C' = (6, 5)
A' = (8, 9)
T' = (9, 6)

ROTATIONS

Rotations spin a shape around a fixed point. This point is called the **centre of rotation**. A shape can turn clockwise OR counter-clockwise from that middle point. If you remember that the centre of rotation itself doesn't move, you'll be fine — promise!

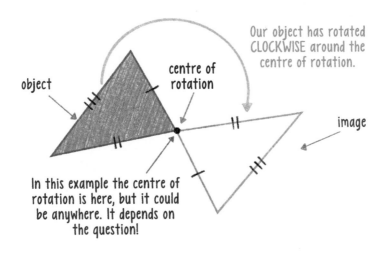

object

centre of rotation

Our object has rotated CLOCKWISE around the centre of rotation.

image

In this example the centre of rotation is here, but it could be anywhere. It depends on the question!

CENTRE OF ROTATION

The centre of rotation might be **on the edge** of a shape, **inside** a shape or **outside** a shape. When it's on the edge or inside, it's like a pin holding the spot and the shape turning from there. When it's outside, it's kind of like you're rotating your shape around an invisible circle whose middle is the centre of rotation. Sort of like a plane circling an airport. Wherever it is, you can move clockwise or counter-clockwise around the centre of rotation.

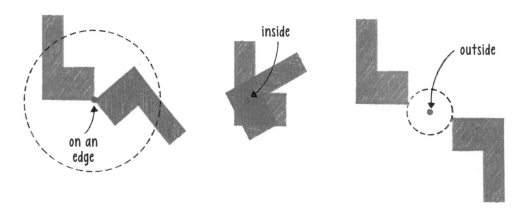

on an edge

inside

outside

Rotations can be hard for EVERYONE — even me — but I have a hack to help. If you're having trouble imagining what a rotation looks like, get crafty! Trace your shape on tracing paper. Cut it out. And then actually turn it around your centre of rotation so you can see what's happening. It's a stepping stone on the road to becoming a rotation pro.

How do we rotate an object?

Right now you probably only need to deal with two types of rotations: 90° rotations and 180° rotations. If you want to be fancy, the amount that we rotate an object is called the **angle of rotation**. A 90° rotation is a quarter of a full turn, and a 180° rotation is a half of a full turn. If you remember that, you're good to go.

Rotating 90° looks like this!

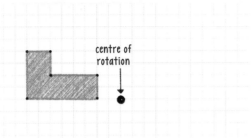

centre of rotation

So, let's check out the centre of rotation. Here, it's located outside the shape.

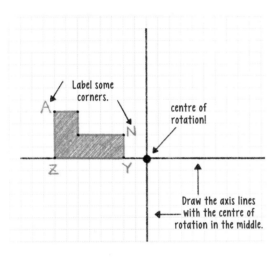

Label some corners.

A

N

centre of rotation!

Z

Y

Draw the axis lines with the centre of rotation in the middle.

Grab a ruler and draw your axis lines, with the centre of rotation in the middle. Now that you've got the four quarters — or quadrants — drawn, it's easier to see how the shape rotates. Label a few key corners — or vertices — so you can see exactly what's happening.

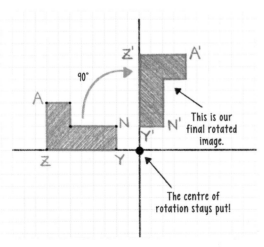

Z'

A'

90°

A

N

N'

Y'

This is our final rotated image.

Z

Y

The centre of rotation stays put!

Rotating 90° means every point gets a quarter of a turn clockwise. Ta-da!

Rotating 180° looks like this!

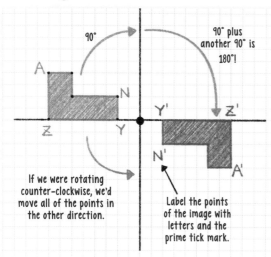

90°

90° plus another 90° is 180°!

A

N

Y'

Z'

Z

Y

N'

A'

If we were rotating counter-clockwise, we'd move all of the points in the other direction.

Label the points of the image with letters and the prime tick mark.

We'll use the same shape and centre of rotation here as the 90° example. A 180° rotation turns all our points over two full quarters, which is the same as one half turn.

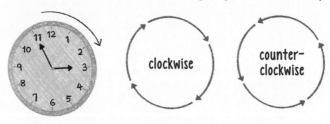

☆ MEMORIZE THIS!

Is it **clockwise** or **counter-clockwise**? Just picture a clock! Clockwise is the same direction that a clock's hands go. "Counter" means "opposite." So, counter-clockwise means that we're going the OTHER way.

clockwise

counter-clockwise

Ready to level up?

Rotating objects using the coordinate system

Your teacher might ask you to rotate a shape using the coordinate system. But don't panic — there are "switch and flip" tricks for that.

Rotate a point 90° clockwise

That means "Hey! **Switch** x and y, then **flip** the sign on the new y!"

If point A is (3, 4), then A prime rotated 90° would be (-4, 3).

Rotate a point 180° clockwise

That means, "Pssst! **Flip** the signs on BOTH x and y!"

If point A is (3, 4), then A prime rotated 180° would be (-3, -4).

LET'S TRY IT!

Q: Graph the image of MEOW after a rotation of 180°.

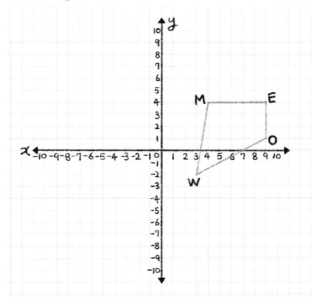

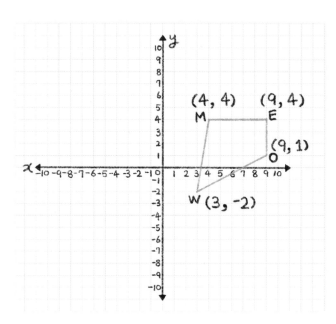

Step 1: Label your coordinates. Every single one of them! Remember, x always comes first in your set, so write them as (x, y).

m (4, 4) → m' = (-4, -4)
E (9, 4) → E' = (-9, -4)
O (9, 1) → O' = (-9, -1)
W (3, -2) → W' = (-3, 2)

Step 2: You've been asked to rotate the shape 180°, and the trick for that is (x, y) → (-x, -y). So, write out all the MEOW points and FLIP THE SIGNS.

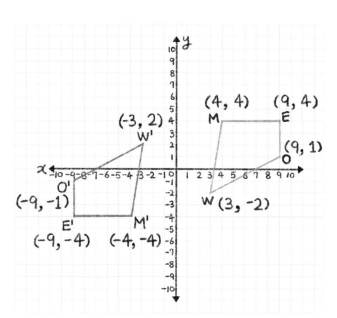

Step 3: Plot your brand-new points to see the brand-new location of your shape, and you are done. OWME! Get it? It's what a cat says after a 180° rotation!

PERIMETER AND AREA
Like Walking around a Field and Mowing It

Perimeter

What even is it?! The distance around the edge of a closed 2-D shape is called its **perimeter**. It is the length of the boundary, or edge, of that 2-D shape. All we do to find the perimeter of any polygon is find the lengths of all of its sides and add them together. And because perimeter is found by adding those side lengths together, we use the same units as when we talk about length. Simple, right?!

FORMULAS FOR FIGURING OUT PERIMETER

What even is a formula?! Sure, we can add every single side length of any shape together to find its perimeter, but there's a quicker way to do it! Knowing simple facts about our favourite shapes allows us to come up with **formulas**. A formula is basically a shortcut to help us calculate faster.

FORMULA ALERT! Perimeter = sum of all sides

☆MEMORIZE THIS!

The best way to memorize a formula is to write it down over and over and over and over. Write each formula down ten times a day for one full week, and I promise it WILL be in your head forever!

Measuring Perimeter

Q: Two sides of this rectangle are 2 cm long, and the other two sides are 4 cm long. Find the perimeter of the shape.

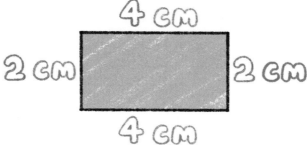

4 cm

2 cm   2 cm

4 cm

LET'S DO IT!

Perimeter = sum of all side lengths

$$P = 2 + 2 + 4 + 4$$

We add all four side lengths together!

$$P = 12 \text{ cm}$$

P stands for perimeter. We use "P" so we don't have to write the whole word out. Remember, IT MATTERS whether our letters in formulas are upper case or lower case!

This is the sum of all of the side lengths.

A: The perimeter of this rectangle is 12 cm.

FAST HACK!

Sometimes we don't NEED to write the entire word for something down, as long as we all agree on a short form for that word. When we're talking about shapes, here are some short forms that Canadian mathematicians have ALL agreed on, so you can use them too!

l = length	A = Area
w = width	P = Perimeter
h = height	
b = base	

FORMULAS FOR COMMON SHAPES

You'll probably need to know how to figure out the perimeter of these shapes. So, let's have a look!

Squares

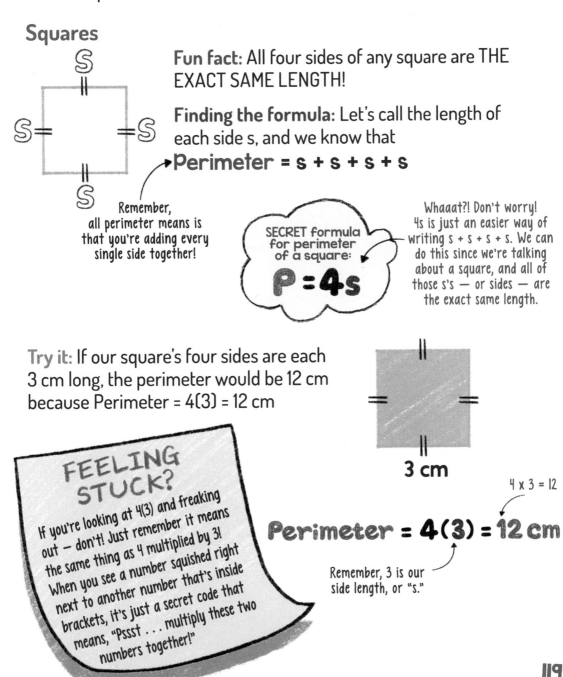

Fun fact: All four sides of any square are THE EXACT SAME LENGTH!

Finding the formula: Let's call the length of each side s, and we know that

Perimeter = s + s + s + s

Remember, all perimeter means is that you're adding every single side together!

SECRET formula for perimeter of a square:

$$P = 4s$$

Whaaat?! Don't worry! 4s is just an easier way of writing s + s + s + s. We can do this since we're talking about a square, and all of those s's — or sides — are the exact same length.

Try it: If our square's four sides are each 3 cm long, the perimeter would be 12 cm because Perimeter = 4(3) = 12 cm

3 cm

FEELING STUCK?

If you're looking at 4(3) and freaking out — don't! Just remember it means the same thing as 4 multiplied by 3! When you see a number squished right next to another number that's inside brackets, it's just a secret code that means, "Pssst . . . multiply these two numbers together!"

4 x 3 = 12

Perimeter = 4(3) = 12 cm

Remember, 3 is our side length, or "s."

Rectangles

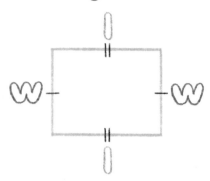

Fun fact: A rectangle has two sides called the lengths (which are of equal length) and two other sides called the widths (which are of equal length).

Finding the formula: Let's call the two longer sides l (for length) and the two shorter sides w (for width).

So, we know **Perimeter** = l + l + w +w

Try it: If our rectangle has two sides that are 4 cm, and two other sides that are 3 cm, the perimeter would be 14 cm because Perimeter = 2(4) + 2(3) = 14 cm

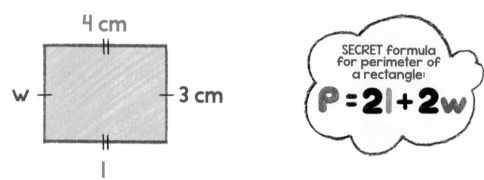

4 cm

w — 3 cm

l

SECRET formula
for perimeter of
a rectangle:

$$P = 2l + 2w$$

$$\text{Perimeter} = 2(4) + 2(3) = 14 \text{ cm}$$

8 + 6 = 14

Our length
is 4.

Our width
is 3.

Parallelograms

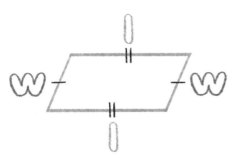

Fun fact: A parallelogram is like a rectangle when it comes to side length: two sides have the same length as each other, and the other two sides have the same length as each other!

Finding the formula: It's the EXACT same as a rectangle. We'll call our two longer sides l (for length) and the two shorter sides w (for width).

So, we know **Perimeter = l + l + w + w**

Try it: If our parallelogram has two sides that are 4 cm, and two other sides that are 2 cm, the perimeter would be 12 cm because Perimeter = 2(4) + 2(2) = 12 cm

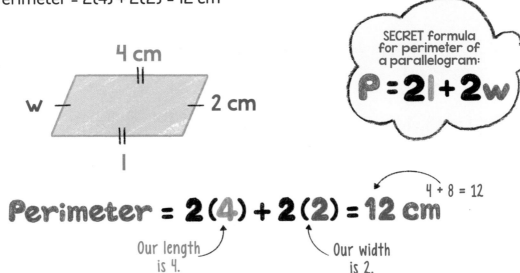

SECRET formula for perimeter of a parallelogram:

$$P = 2l + 2w$$

$$\text{Perimeter} = 2(4) + 2(2) = 12 \text{ cm}$$

4 + 8 = 12

Our length is 4.

Our width is 2.

Triangles

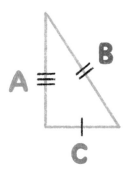

Fun fact: This formula for scalene triangles works for all triangles. It doesn't matter if they are equilateral, scalene or isosceles!

Finding the formula for scalene (or any!) triangles: Let's call the three sides **A**, **B** and **C** — since they're all totally different, they all need totally different letters! So, we know that **Perimeter = sA + sB + sC**

Try it: If the triangle's sides are 3 cm, 4 cm and 5 cm, the perimeter would be 9 cm because Perimeter = 4 + 5 + 3 = 12

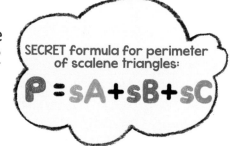

SECRET formula for perimeter of scalene triangles:

$$P = sA + sB + sC$$

$$P = 4 + 5 + 3 = 12 \text{ cm}$$

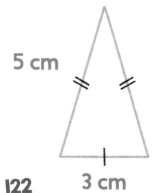

5 cm

4 cm

3 cm

Finding the formula for isosceles triangles: Isosceles triangles have two sides that are the SAME LENGTH, so **Perimeter = 2s + b**

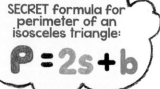

SECRET formula for perimeter of an isosceles triangle:

$$P = 2s + b$$

Try it: If our triangle had two sides that were each 5 cm long and one side that was 3 cm long, the perimeter would be 13 cm because Perimeter = 2(5) + 3 = 13 cm

$$P = 2(5) + 3 = 13 \text{ cm}$$

5 cm

3 cm

122

Finding the formula for equilateral triangles: Equilateral triangles have three sides that are ALL the SAME LENGTH, so

Perimeter = s + s + s

SECRET formula for perimeter of an equilateral triangle:
$$P = 3s$$

Try it: If our triangle's three sides are each 2 cm long, the perimeter would be 6 cm because Perimeter = 3(2) = 6 cm

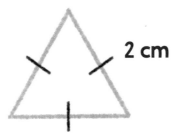 2 cm $P = 3(2) = 6$ cm

Ready to level up?

Sometimes you know part of a shape's perimeter — and then you're asked to go on a hunt for the missing side lengths. Ready?

LET'S TRY IT!

Q: Find the missing side lengths in this rectangle.

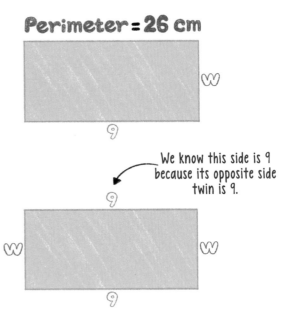

Perimeter = 26 cm

w

9

We know this side is 9 because its opposite side twin is 9.

9

w   w

9

Step 1: Remember your rectangle rules! In a rectangle, the opposite sides are twins. So, let's fill in what we know. You can fill in 9 on the top and w on the left because of the twins rule. So, now you really only have the length of two sides missing . . . and they're identical twins, so that makes things easier!

Step 2: Now, let's talk perimeter. Start with the formula for the perimeter of a rectangle. Then, fill in what you know!

$$P = 2l + 2w$$

Remember, 26 is our perimeter, so we replace P with 26 in our formula.

$$26 = 2(9) + 2w$$

9 is the length.

$$26 = (18) + 2w$$

Step 3: You know that all sides add up to 26. And you know that those two long sides take up 18 of those 26 cm. So, let's subtract 18 from 26 to see how much perimeter there is LEFT to spread across the two shorter sides!

$$26 - 18 = 8$$

Step 4: You got it! Since you have 8 cm of perimeter left, and two sides that need to share it, all you do is divide 8 by 2 to find out what each gets!

$$8 \div 2$$

Ta-DA! Each w gets 4 cm, which means

A: The missing side length is 4 cm.

In math it's important to understand WHY things are the way they are, but it's also important to memorize certain things. That way they're just there in your brain when you need them quickly. If you understand how each formula works, it'll be easier to remember. Trust me on this: understand first and memorize second.

Area

What even is it?! The amount of space covered by a 2-D shape is called its **area**. Remember, perimeter is the distance along the outside edge of a shape, and area is the space INSIDE that shape!

How do we measure area? We measure area in square units. What that means is we write down the unit we're using to measure all of our lengths, and then put a teeny 2 beside and a bit above the last letter of the unit we're using, like this: cm^2 or m^2 or km^2.

> *Fancy Lingo!*
>
> That little 2 is what we call an **exponent**. Use THAT word in class and get pumped to turn heads!

WAIT — What even IS a square unit? Check out this piece of yummy chocolate. One side is 1 cm long — we call that its length. The other side is 1 cm wide — we call that its width. A square that is 1 cm long and 1 cm wide covers an area of $1\,cm^2$!

width 1cm *length 1cm*

$1cm^2$ is the area covered.

PRO TIP! If each side were 1 m long, it would be 1 square metre, or $1\,m^2$. You can do this with ANY unit used to measure length!

Now, imagine we wanted to make a BIGGER chocolate bar with even more squares. So, we line them up by placing two squares side by side, three times. If we look at the length, the chocolate bar is 3 cm long. Its width is 2 cm. If we count all of the squares, this bar contains 6 square centimetres of chocolate, so its area is 6 cm².

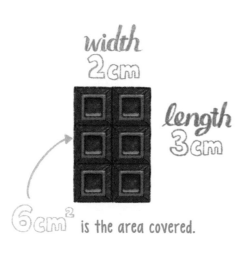

width
2cm

length
3cm

6cm² is the area covered.

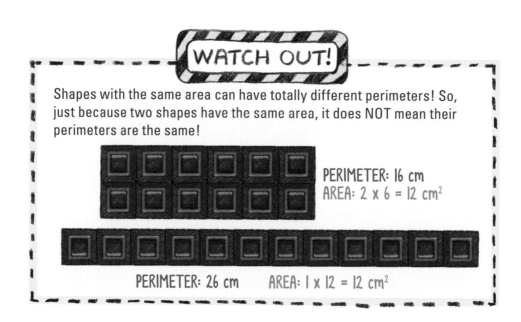

WATCH OUT!

Shapes with the same area can have totally different perimeters! So, just because two shapes have the same area, it does NOT mean their perimeters are the same!

PERIMETER: 16 cm
AREA: 2 x 6 = 12 cm²

PERIMETER: 26 cm   AREA: 1 x 12 = 12 cm²

AREA FORMULAS FOR COMMON SHAPES!

While it's cool to just count the number of square units in a shape, it doesn't always work perfectly. Squares don't fit nicely into all shapes — think of a triangle! A better method is to use formulas, just like we do for perimeter. And, just like the perimeter formulas, let's understand WHY our formula for each shape makes sense.

Squares & Rectangles

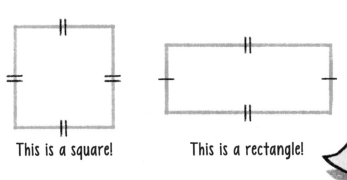

This is a square!   This is a rectangle!

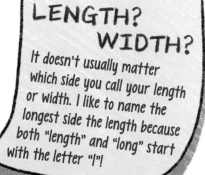

LENGTH? WIDTH?

It doesn't usually matter which side you call your length or width. I like to name the longest side the length because both "length" and "long" start with the letter "l"!

Finding the formula: If you know the length and width of a rectangle or square, just multiply them together to find its area. **Area = length × width**

SECRET formula for area of a square or rectangle:

$$A = l \times w$$

Try it: If the length of our rectangle is 5 cm and its width is 2 cm, then its area would be 10 cm^2 because . . .

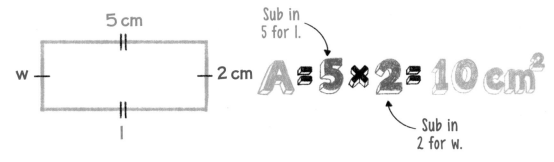

5 cm

w   2 cm

l

Sub in 5 for l.

$$A = 5 \times 2 = 10 \text{ cm}^2$$

Sub in 2 for w.

Parallelograms

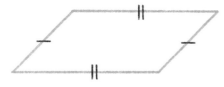

Finding the formula: Copy this parallelogram accurately onto a piece of paper, cut it out, and then follow the steps below:

To find the height, draw a line segment that starts at the top vertex and is perpendicular to the base. Remember, perpendicular means it makes a 90° angle with the base!

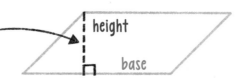

height

base

1) Cut here.

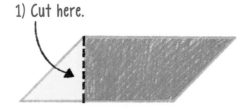

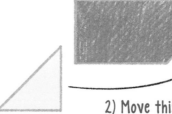

2) Move this triangle here.

TA-DA! The shape you have made is a rectangle! So, you can just use the same formula we use to find the area of a rectangle — with one BIG difference. Instead of using the words "length" and "width," we use the words "**base**" and "**height**."

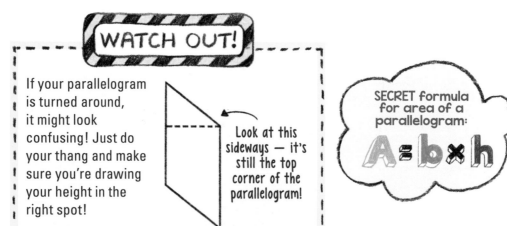

WATCH OUT!

If your parallelogram is turned around, it might look confusing! Just do your thang and make sure you're drawing your height in the right spot!

Look at this sideways — it's still the top corner of the parallelogram!

SECRET formula for area of a parallelogram:

$A = b \times h$

Try it: If the base of our parallelogram is 5 cm and its height is 2 cm, then its area would be 10 cm² because . . .

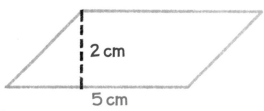

2 cm

5 cm

$$A = 5 \times 2 = 10 \text{ cm}^2$$

Triangles

Finding the formula: This time, picture cutting a parallelogram diagonally, from corner to corner. If you did that, you would get TWO identical triangles. So, if we figure out the area of that parallelogram and then divide it by 2, we'll get the area of one of those triangles! How cool is that?!

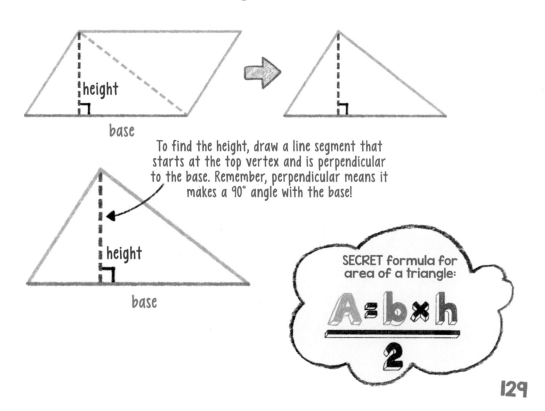

height

base

To find the height, draw a line segment that starts at the top vertex and is perpendicular to the base. Remember, perpendicular means it makes a 90° angle with the base!

height

base

SECRET formula for area of a triangle:

$$A = \frac{b \times h}{2}$$

Try it: If the base of our triangle is 6 cm and its height is 3 cm, then its area would be 9 cm² because . . .

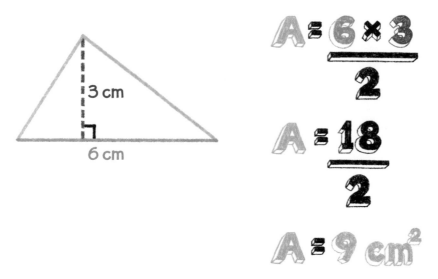

$$A = \frac{6 \times 3}{2}$$

$$A = \frac{18}{2}$$

$$A = 9 \text{ cm}^2$$

Finding the formula for right-angle triangles: Okay, so these guys are special because you can already SEE their height! Remember, you have a right-angle triangle when one of the sides hits the other side at a 90° angle, making a perfect L shape. The vertical side that intersects with the base to make the 90° angle IS its height, so you can just use that!

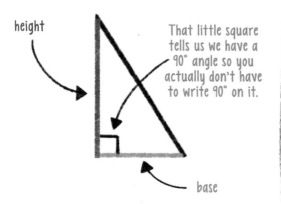

height

That little square tells us we have a 90° angle so you actually don't have to write 90° on it.

base

Think Of It THIS Way!

Your teacher might write the formula for the area of a triangle differently, like this:

Area = b x height ÷ 2

or

A = b x h ÷ 2

or

A = ½ x b x h

Remember that cutting in half is the same thing as dividing by 2. All three formulas mean the exact same thing, so just use the one you like best!

SURFACE AREA AND VOLUME

Getting Down with the Third Dimension

This whole chapter is about how shapes POP in real life. That's right — we're talking about 3-D! Have you ever been to a 3-D movie? The screen is FLAT, but when you put on those cool 3-D glasses, everything seems to jump out of it. Well, that's what we're talking about right here. In real life, shapes ARE usually 3-D. When we talk about the nature of a 3-D shape, we're usually thinking about its **surface area** (the amount of "outside" a shape has) OR its **volume** (the amount of "inside" it has). Are you ready for a wild ride into ANOTHER DIMENSION?

SURFACE AREA

What even is it?! The outside of a 3-D shape is called its **surface**. For example, the surface of a box of cereal is the cardboard part. We can think of surface area as, like, a cozy blanket that wraps all around the surface of the object.

How do we figure out surface area? Surface area is the sum of the areas of all of the shapes that cover a 3-D object's outside. Think of that cereal box — it's just made up of a bunch of rectangles. So, you find the area of each side, then add them all together. If you need a refresher on calculating area of 2-D shapes, flip back a chapter. After that, it's just addition, so you got this! And just like 2-D area, we measure surface area in square units, using a RULER. It is THE must-have tool for measuring ANYTHING with straight lines.

SURFACE AREA FORMULAS FOR COMMON SHAPES

Common shapes are those basic ones we see all the time. We can figure out surface area using the power of formulas — they're the BEST hacks! But first, you need to understand how the formulas work. And just like with all formulas, it's SUPER IMPORTANT to use the universal language of math. Pay attention to whether the letters in your formulas are upper case or lower case.

FAST HACK!

Sometimes we don't NEED to write the entire word for something down, as long as we all agree on a short form for that word. When we're talking about shapes, here are some short forms that Canadian mathematicians have ALL agreed on, so you can use them too!

l = length	SA = Surface Area
w = width	V = Volume
h = height	
b = base	

Rectangular Prisms

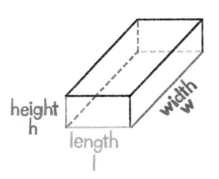

height
h

length
l

width
w

Fun Fact: These have six faces. Each face is either a rectangle or a square, which are both shapes you already know how to find the area of. Remember A = l x w?

Finding the formula: If you take a good look at a rectangular prism, you can see it's made up of three pairs of shapes. Find the area of each unique shape, and multiply that number by 2 (since there are two of each). Do that for each of the three pairs, then add the three totals together and THAT is our surface area!

It looks like this: **Surface Area = 2 x length x width + 2 x length x height + 2 x width x height**

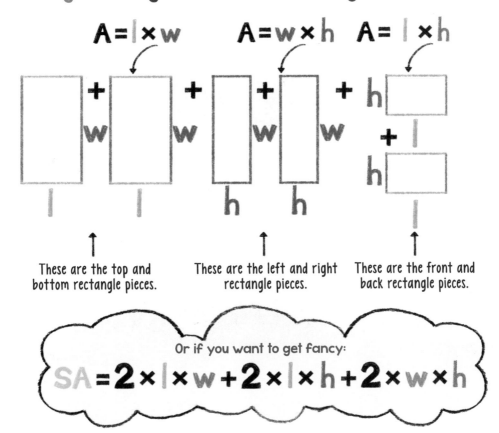

$$A = l \times w \qquad A = w \times h \qquad A = l \times h$$

These are the top and bottom rectangle pieces.

These are the left and right rectangle pieces.

These are the front and back rectangle pieces.

Or if you want to get fancy:

$$SA = 2 \times l \times w + 2 \times l \times h + 2 \times w \times h$$

133

Try it! If our rectangular prism's length was 3 cm, its width 5 cm and its height 1 cm, then its surface area would be 62 cm² because:

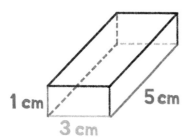

$$SA = 2 \times l \times w + 2 \times l \times h + 2 \times w \times h$$
$$SA = 2 \times 3 \times 5 + 2 \times 3 \times 1 + 2 \times 5 \times 1$$
$$SA = 2 \times 15 + 6 + 10$$
$$SA = 46 \text{ cm}^2$$

Cubes

Fun fact: A cube is a special rectangular prism where every single one of its edges is the same length. This means each of its faces has the same area.

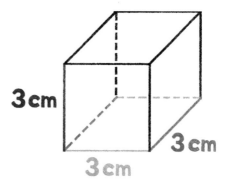

Finding the formula: All we have to do is find the area of ONE face, then multiply it by 6, since there are six of them! And since a cube's length and width are the same, you can grab any measurement and go for it.

Surface Area $= 6 \times$ **length** $\times$ **width**

Try it! If the cube's side length is 3 cm, then its surface area would be 54 cm² because:

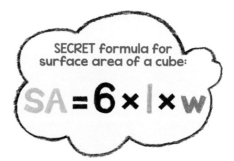

SECRET formula for surface area of a cube:

$$SA = 6 \times l \times w$$

$$SA = 6 \times l \times w$$
$$SA = 6 \times 3 \times 3$$
$$SA = 6 \times 9$$
$$SA = 54 \text{ cm}^2$$

Or if you want to get fancy:

$$SA = 6 \times side^2$$

Triangular Prisms

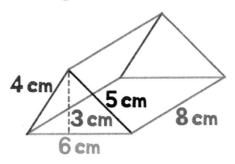

Fun fact: A triangular prism has two identical-twin end faces that are — you guessed it — triangles. But the other three shapes in a triangular prism are rectangles.

Finding the formula: Just break it down! We've got two matching triangles and three rectangles, so five shapes in total. Find the area of each shape, and add the amounts together.

Surface Area **= Area of triangle + Area of triangle + Area of bottom rectangle + Area of first side rectangle + Area of second side rectangle**

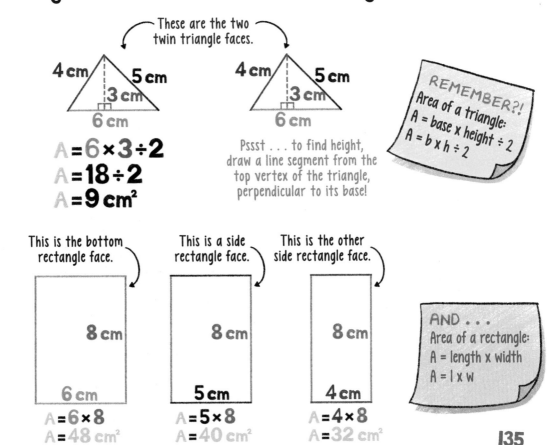

These are the two twin triangle faces.

$A = 6 \times 3 \div 2$
$A = 18 \div 2$
$A = 9 \text{ cm}^2$

Pssst . . . to find height, draw a line segment from the top vertex of the triangle, perpendicular to its base!

REMEMBER?!
Area of a triangle:
$A = \text{base} \times \text{height} \div 2$
$A = b \times h \div 2$

This is the bottom rectangle face.

This is a side rectangle face.

This is the other side rectangle face.

$A = 6 \times 8$
$A = 48 \text{ cm}^2$

$A = 5 \times 8$
$A = 40 \text{ cm}^2$

$A = 4 \times 8$
$A = 32 \text{ cm}^2$

AND . . .
Area of a rectangle:
$A = \text{length} \times \text{width}$
$A = l \times w$

135

Now, we just add all the pieces up!

Surface Area $= 9 + 9 + 48 + 40 + 32 = 138 \text{ cm}^2$

SECRET formula for surface area of a triangular prism:

$$SA = \frac{1}{2} \times b \times h + \frac{1}{2} \times b \times h + l \times w + l \times w + l \times w$$

USING NETS TO FIND SURFACE AREA

Another way you can deal with surface area is by using a net — that's a 3-D shape that's been all flattened out so you can see each face of the figure. Think back to our cereal box. If you separate it at the seams (umm, eat the cereal first!), you can see all of the shapes laid out. And you can even fold it all back together to be 3-D again.

Rectangular Prism Net

Let's find the surface area of this rectangular prism!

Step 1: First, flatten it out into a net so YOU can see all of the shapes.

Check out the measurements for each edge and see where they match up to the 3-D shape.

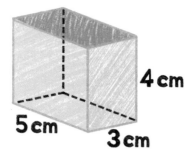

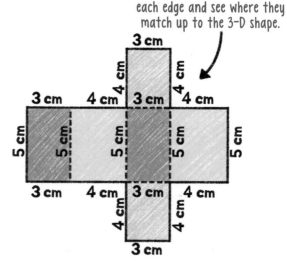

Step 2: Find the area of the purple rectangles — it's l x w x 2, since there are two of them!
A = 5 x 3 x 2
A = 30 cm²

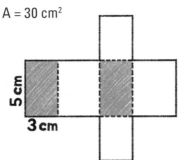

Step 3: Next up, do the area of the green rectangles.
A = 5 x 4 x 2
A = 40 cm²

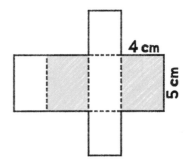

Step 4: Then — you guessed it! — the blue rectangles.
A = 4 x 3 x 2
A = 24 cm²

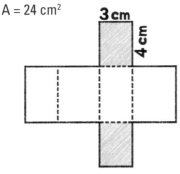

Step 5: Finally, add all of those areas together to find the surface area!
SA = 30 + 40 + 24
SA = 94cm²

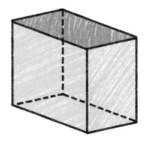

Triangular Prism Net

Let's find the surface area of this triangular prism!

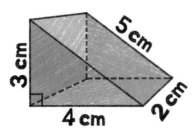

Step 1: First, flatten it out into a net so you can see all of the shapes.

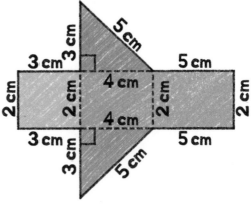

137

Step 2: Find the area of the orange rectangle.

$A = 4 \times 2$

$A = 8 \text{ cm}^2$

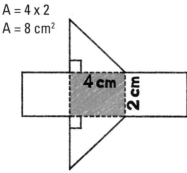

Step 3: Next, calculate the area of the green rectangle on the left.

$A = 3 \times 2$

$A = 6 \text{ cm}^2$

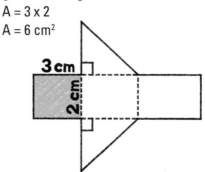

Step 4: Next, calculate the area of the purple rectangle on the right.

$A = 5 \times 2$

$A = 10 \text{ cm}^2$

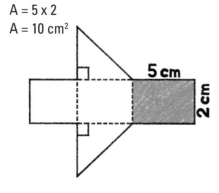

Step 5: Now, the area of the triangles. They're identical, so just find the area of one of them and then multiply that by two.

$A = \dfrac{3 \times 4}{2} \times 2$

$A = \dfrac{12}{2} \times 2$

$A = 12 \text{ cm}^2$

Pssst! See that little square? This is a right triangle, so the height is 3 cm!

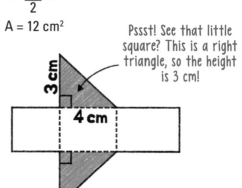

Step 6: Finally, add all of those areas together to find the surface area!

$SA = 8 + 6 + 10 + 12$

$SA = 36 \text{ cm}^2$

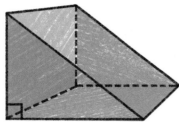

Volume

What even is it?! The amount of space a 3-D shape takes up is called its **volume**. We can also think of volume as the amount of stuff that can FILL or fit inside of a 3-D shape. For example, with a swimming pool, we can think of the amount of SPACE that a swimming pool takes up, but we can also think of the amount of water that could fit inside the pool.

COOL Fact!

IRL, we can fill a 3-D object with three types of stuff: liquids, gases or solids. Just imagine a balloon, a can of pop or a box of cereal.

VOLUME OF SOLIDS AND GASES

What even is it?! When we're using volume to talk about solids or gases, we're talking about how much space a given 3-D shape takes up instead of how much stuff is inside it.

How do we measure the volume of solids?

We measure volume in **cubic units**. It's the same unit we're using to measure length, but it's going 3-D! We take the unit — say, centimetres — and then put a teeny 3 up at the end when we write it, like this: cm^3. You'd read that as "centimetre cubed."

Wait, what even IS a cubic unit? Check out this super-chill ice cube. One side is 1 cm long — that's the length. One side is 1 cm wide — that's the width. One side is 1 cm high — that's the height. This cool cube is 1 cubic centimetre, and the volume it contains is 1 cm^3!

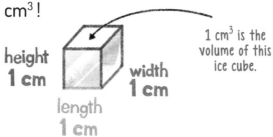

height
1 cm

width
1 cm

length
1 cm

1 cm^3 is the volume of this ice cube.

Units unite! If each side were 1 m long, this cube would be 1 cubic metre, or 1 m^3. If they were 1 km long, it would be 1 cubic kilometre, or 1 km^3. You can do the same thing with ANY unit used to measure length!

Now, imagine we wanted to make a bigger block of ice out of more of those cubes. Let's line them up, placing three of them in a row, two times. And we'll put another identical layer of ice cubes on top of that first one. We can see that if we were to measure the length of the ice block we've made, it would be 3 cm long. Its width would be 2 cm. And its height would also be 2 cm. But we can also see, by counting the ice cubes, that our ice block contains 12 of those cubed centimetre ice cubes, so its volume is 12 cm^3!

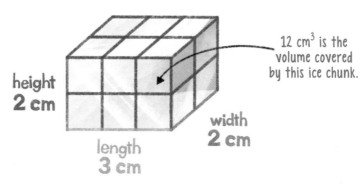

height
2 cm

length
3 cm

width
2 cm

12 cm^3 is the volume covered by this ice chunk.

VOLUME FORMULAS FOR COMMON SHAPES

Instead of counting each cube, you could have used an awesome FORMULA and instantly had your answer! Formulas, those super-handy calculation shortcuts, help us to figure out the volume when squares won't fit nicely into a shape. But first, let's understand WHY the formula for each shape makes sense. Then, let's memorize them so we can quickly remember them when we need to calculate the area of any shape!

Rectangular Prisms

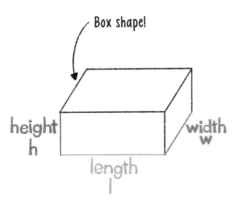

Box shape!

height
h

width
w

length
l

Fun facts: A rectangular prism is any box-shaped 3-D object made of six rectangles. Remember that a square is a special kind of rectangle, so this formula works for cubes too!

Finding the formula: If you know the length, width and height of a rectangular prism, all you have to do is find the area of its base and multiply that by the height of the 3-D shape!

Volume = area of base x height of 3-D shape

And since we know the base is a rectangle AND that the formula for the area of a rectangle is length x width, we can make it even simpler . . .

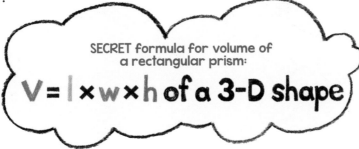

SECRET formula for volume of a rectangular prism:

$$V = l \times w \times h \text{ of a 3-D shape}$$

Try it! If the length of our rectangular base is 5 cm, its width is 4 cm, and the height of the 3-D shape is 2 cm, then the volume of our rectangular prism would be 40 cm³ because:

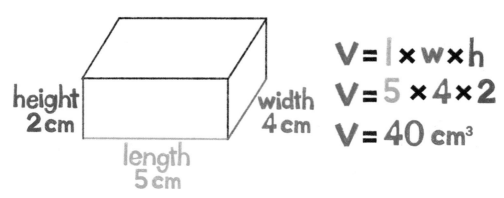

$$V = l \times w \times h$$
$$V = 5 \times 4 \times 2$$
$$V = 40 \text{ cm}^3$$

Cool cubes!

A cube is a special rectangular prism where every single one of its edges is the same length. That means finding its volume is super easy! You only need to find the length of one side, then multiply that number by itself twice!

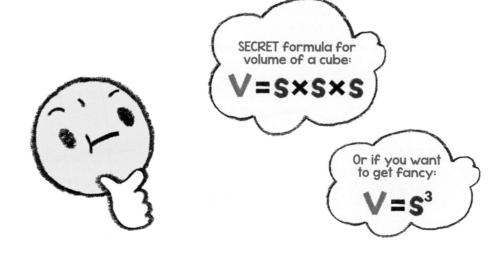

SECRET formula for volume of a cube:

$$V = s \times s \times s$$

Or if you want to get fancy:

$$V = s^3$$

Triangular Prisms

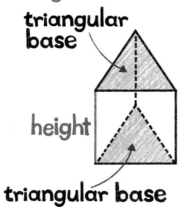

triangular base

height

triangular base

Fun fact: A triangular prism has two identical end faces — called the bases — that are triangles. The height of a triangular prism is the length between those two bases, no matter which way they are facing!

Finding the formula: If you know how to find the volume of a rectangular prism, you're halfway to doing it for a triangular one. The difference is that you need to find the area of a triangular base instead of one that's a rectangle! And OF COURSE the formula for the area of a triangle is base x height ÷ 2, so . . .

Volume = area of base × height of prism

Try it! If the height of our 3-D shape is 6 cm, the base of our triangle is 4 cm, and the height of our triangle is 3 cm, then its volume would be 36 cm^3 because:

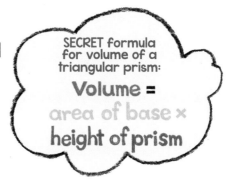

SECRET formula for volume of a triangular prism:

Volume = area of base × height of prism

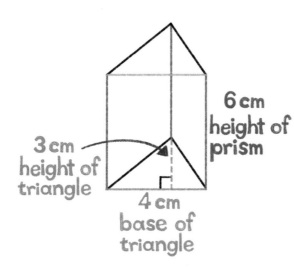

6 cm height of prism

3 cm height of triangle

4 cm base of triangle

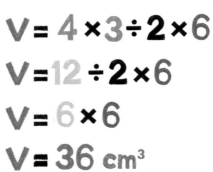

$V = 4 \times 3 \div 2 \times 6$

$V = 12 \div 2 \times 6$

$V = 6 \times 6$

$V = 36 \text{ cm}^3$

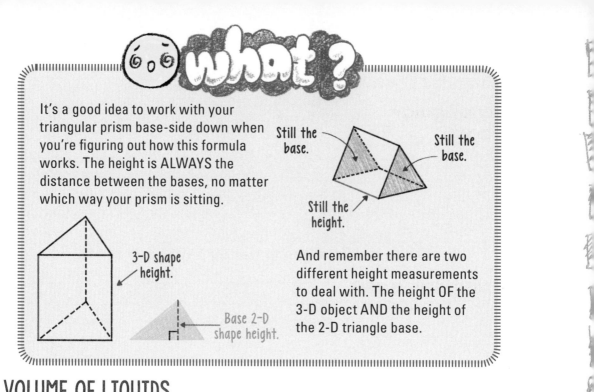

It's a good idea to work with your triangular prism base-side down when you're figuring out how this formula works. The height is ALWAYS the distance between the bases, no matter which way your prism is sitting.

Still the base.

Still the base.

Still the height.

3-D shape height.

Base 2-D shape height.

And remember there are two different height measurements to deal with. The height OF the 3-D object AND the height of the 2-D triangle base.

VOLUME OF LIQUIDS

What even is it!? When we're using volume to talk about liquids, we're talking about the amount of stuff we can FILL a 3-D shape with! Sometimes this is called its **capacity**.

How do we measure volume of liquids? In Canada, volume is measured in metric units. There are lots of units in the metric system, but here are the ones you'll be dealing with most.

Millilitres: Use this to measure small quantities of liquid, like a glass of water. One millilitre is actually the exact amount of water that would fill a 1 cm x 1 cm x 1 cm cube. You'd need 5 mL of water to fill up a teaspoon. A juice box is about 200 mL!

Litres: Use this unit for measuring larger quantities of liquid, like the amount needed to fill a giant fish tank. One litre is about the same amount of liquid as there is in a tall carton of chocolate milk.

CONVERTING BETWEEN UNITS OF VOLUME

It's super easy to switch between our units of volume — thanks, metric system! To convert litres into millilitres, we multiply by 1000. To convert from millilitres to litres, we divide by 1000!

From BIG units to SMALLER units

LITRES to MILLILITRES
×1000

1L   1000 mL

MILLILITRES to LITRES
÷1000

From SMALL units to BIGGER units

SHORT FORMS!
These super-fast short forms are used a lot.
millilitres → mL (or ml)
litres → L

Think Of It THIS Way!

Why do we care about converting from one unit to another? Well, because to compare amounts, or add things together, or do ANY calculation, the measurements HAVE to be in the same unit. Think about it: Would you rather have 1 L of chocolate milk to share with your BFF or 900 mL? Nine hundred sounds like more than 1 — but is it? How do you even know unless you compare using the same unit?

DOING ACTUAL MATH WITH VOLUME

What do we even do with volume? Well, we can compare, add and subtract different volumes, just like we've been doing with other numbers. But first you HAVE to convert those units.

Q: Would you rather have 900 mL or 1 L of chocolate milk to share with your BFF?

Big unit (litres) to small unit (millilitres)

$$1 \times 1000 = 1000$$
1000 mL is more than 900 mL

or

Small unit (millilitres) to big unit (litres)

$$900 \div 1000 = 0.9$$
0.9 L is still less than 1 L!

A: You totally want 1 L for maximum chocolatey goodness.

 Is it supposed to be ml or mL? Both are correct, but sometimes it's good to use mL so the pesky l doesn't get confused for a 1. That's why we're going to do that here. But you should TOTALLY check with your teacher for which way they prefer.

LET'S TRY IT!

Q: You want to make a sparkling punch. Your pitcher has a capacity of 3 L. Is it big enough to hold 2 L of ginger ale and 750 mL of fruit juice? What volume of punch will that make?

All you have to do is add the volumes of the liquids together and compare that to the volume the pitcher holds. But WAIT! You need to make sure all of our units are the same before comparing or calculating them.

Recipe calls for 750 mL of juice . . .

. . . and 2 L of ginger ale.

Step 1: First, pick the unit you want everything to be measured in. Let's go with litres because that's the capacity of the pitcher. The ginger ale is already in litres, so cool. You need to figure out how many litres the juice is, so that you can calculate the amount of fruit punch in the same units.

To change millilitres into litres, just divide the number of millilitres you have by 1000.

$$750 \div 1000 = 0.75 \text{ L}$$

Step 2: Now all you have to do is add the two amounts together!

$$2 + 0.75 = 2.75 \text{ L}$$

A: There is a total of 2.75 L of fruit punch. Since the pitcher has a capacity of 3 L, and 3 > 2.75, you can use it for your punch. There's even room for ice!

MASS

Lighten Up — It's Just Math!

What even is it?! **Mass** is the measure of how HEAVY the stuff that makes up an object is. But don't mix it up with volume, which is the measure of how much SPACE that stuff takes up. So, the volume of an apple is a measure of how much space that apple takes up, but the mass of an apple is how HEAVY that apple is.

Watch out for these keywords! If you see these magic words, they're probably talking about measuring mass.

MEASURING MASS

How do we measure mass? We measure mass and weight with a scale. There are lots of different types of scales. Bathroom scales weigh people, kitchen scales weigh food and balance scales are often found in classrooms. Like length, we usually measure mass in metric units. The most common units for measuring mass are:

Milligrams: We use these for measuring things that are super light, like how much a small feather weighs. One milligram is about the mass of a tiny ant. Short form: **mg**

Grams: Go to grams for measuring things that are light, like how heavy an apple is. One gram is about the mass of a jelly bean. Short form: **g**

Kilograms: These are used for measuring things that are a bit heavier, like how heavy a puppy is. One kilogram is about the mass of a pineapple. Short form: **kg**

Metric tonnes: If you need to measure things that are SUPER-duper heavy, like a bus, you'll want to use tonnes. One tonne is about the mass of a bull. Short form: **t**

what?

A lot of people think mass and weight are the same thing, but they're not! Mass is the amount of stuff an object is made of. It doesn't matter WHERE that object is . . . Even if it's on the moon, its mass stays the same. But WEIGHT is different. Weight measures how heavy something is when it's being pulled down by gravity. Gravity changes from planet to planet. As the force of gravity increases or decreases, so does an object's weight. For example, if you weigh 32 kg on Earth, you'd weigh 12 kg on Mercury, where the pull of gravity is less. On Earth, an object's mass and weight are the same. But anywhere else in the solar system, that object's mass and weight would be different numbers!

Mass in Action!

CONVERTING BETWEEN COMMON UNITS OF MASS

It's super easy to convert from one unit of mass to another. Each unit "fits" into the next-biggest unit 1000 times. So, all we have to do is multiply or divide by 1000 to convert from one unit to another. Like this . . .

From BIG units to SMALL units: multiply ✕

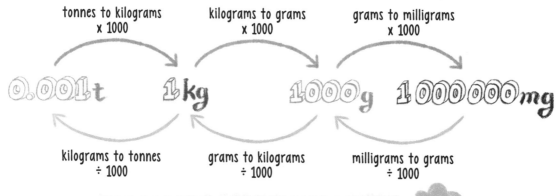

| tonnes to kilograms | kilograms to grams | grams to milligrams |
| x 1000 | x 1000 | x 1000 |

0.001 t   1 kg   1000 g   1 000 000 mg

| kilograms to tonnes | grams to kilograms | milligrams to grams |
| ÷ 1000 | ÷ 1000 | ÷ 1000 |

From SMALL units to BIG units: ÷ divide

Learn This by Heart!

1 t = 1000 kg   1 kg = 1000 g   1 g = 1000 mg

DOING ACTUAL MATH WITH MASS

What do we even do with mass? Well, we can add, subtract, divide and multiply with mass just like we've been doing with other numbers — there's not much more to it. Just remember that all of your measurements have to be in the same unit, and then do any calculations you want! Remember, mass is just a bunch of numbers, so treat it the same way you would anything else.

> **Q:** It's a sleepover, and you're making chocolate-chip cookies with your BFF. The recipe calls for 500 g of chocolate chips. You put your pile of chocolate chips on a scale, and it says you have 0.4 kg of chocolate chips. You're confused! Do you have enough for your recipe? If not, how much more do you need?

We know there are TWO questions here, because there are TWO question marks! Let's start by answering the first question: Do you have enough chocolate chips?

> **ZERO IS A HERO!**
> When you're working with decimals, use zero when you don't have a number to the left of your decimal point. 0.4 looks way nicer than .4 and makes it clear your dot is a decimal point.

Step 1: To figure this out, you first need to make sure ALL of your units are the same. Change your 0.4 kg into g. You could also change your g into kg and that would be okay too. Just pick the unit you want everything to be measured in, and change everything into THAT unit.

To change kilograms into grams, all you do is multiply the number of kilograms you have by 1000.

$$0.4 \times 1000 = 400 \text{ g}$$

Step 2: Now that you've done that, do you have the 500 g of chocolate chips the recipe asked for? NO!

Step 3: Now you can answer the second question: How much more do you need? To figure this out, all you have to do is subtract the smaller mass from the larger mass. So, you subtract 400 from 500!

$$500 - 400 = 100 \text{ g}$$

A: You don't have enough chocolate chips! You need 100 g more so that you can make your cookies!

WATCH OUT!

If you want full marks, always remember to include the unit of measurement that's in the question! Otherwise the answer could be anything. In this case, 100 what? Freckles? Bunnies? Bananas? NO, silly! It's 100 GRAMS of chocolate chips!

SYSTEMS OF MEASUREMENT FOR MASS

Just like with length, in Canada we usually measure mass in metric units. But imperial units of mass are still part of our lives. For example, you probably know your weight in pounds, right? Well, pounds are part of the imperial system, which is what is used in the United States. It's good to understand how metric and imperial measure up to each other.

Here are some of the imperial units you may have come across and their conversions to the metric system:

Ounces	Pounds	Tons
1 ounce = 28 grams	1 pound = 0.45 kilograms	1 ton = 0.9 tonnes

CONVERTING POUNDS INTO KILOGRAMS

Pounds seem to come up a lot, so here's a hack to convert back and forth between kilograms and pounds! The short form for pounds is lb, and OF COURSE kg is the abbreviation for kilograms.

1 kilogram equals about 2.2 pounds.
To convert from **kg** to **lb**, multiply your **kg** value by 2.2.

kg → lb = kg × 2.2

1 pound equals approximately 0.45 kilograms.
To convert from **lb** to **kg**, multiply the **lb** value by 0.45.

lb → kg = lb × 0.45

Let's try it in real life!

> **Q:** How many kg is 271 lbs, rounded to the nearest full kilogram?

Step 1: Remember the conversion: 1 pound is about 0.45 kilograms. So, that's 271 x 0.45. BUT, when you're multiplying by decimals, ditch them at the beginning. You'll add them back at the end. So your problem looks like:

$$271 \times 45$$

Step 2: Write the number with the most digits at the top and the one with fewer underneath it. Digits with the same place value must be directly on top of one another. Remember to label your place values!

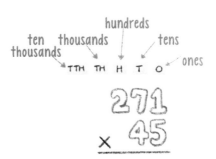

MULTIPLICATION MATTERS!
Remember when I was saying how learning was like building an ice-cream sundae? (See page 21!) Multiplication is one of those important scoops of foundation ice cream, so here's a cool refresher!

Step 3: Multiply each of the digits on the top row by 5 — the number on the bottom row. Start on the right with the ones column, and do ONE column at a time, moving left. So you're multiplying 1 times 5 ones, giving you 5. Stick that 5 under the line in the ones column then move to the next digit on the left.

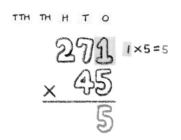

TTH TH H T O

$1 \times 5 = 5$

Step 4: Next, multiply the 5 by the 7 tens. That gives you 35 tens. Write the 5 under the line in the tens column. Carry the 3 over to the hundreds column by marking a little 3 up there.

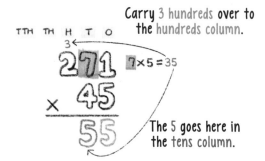

Carry 3 hundreds over to the hundreds column.

TTH TH H T O

$7 \times 5 = 35$

The 5 goes here in the tens column.

Step 5: Next, multiply the 5 by the 2 hundreds. You know that 2 x 5 = 10, but remember: you have that extra 3 you carried over from the last step, so add that on, giving you 13 hundreds. Write the 3 under the line in the hundreds column and the 1 under the line in the thousands column.

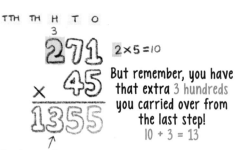

TTH TH H T O

$2 \times 5 = 10$

But remember, you have that extra 3 hundreds you carried over from the last step!

$10 + 3 = 13$

The 3 goes here in the hundreds column. Put the 1 next door in the thousands column.

Step 6: Time to start a brand-new row under the one you just completed so you can multiply all the digits in the top row by 4 tens! Before you start, stick a 0 in the ones column. Just do it! That zero will help you keep track of your place values. Next, cross out any little numbers you carried over from previous steps, so you don't get confused. But don't erase them — you want to be able to trace your steps!

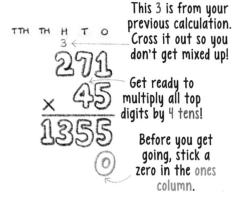

This 3 is from your previous calculation. Cross it out so you don't get mixed up!

TTH TH H T O

Get ready to multiply all top digits by 4 tens!

Before you get going, stick a zero in the ones column.

Step 7: Multiply 4 tens by 1 one. The answer is 4 tens, so just put your 4 below the line, in the tens column. Think of it this way: you're putting your 4 in the first available spot to the left of the zero — that's it!

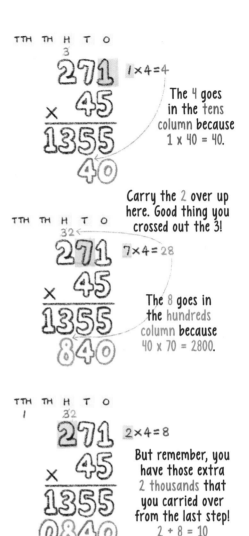

$1 \times 4 = 4$

The 4 goes in the tens column because $1 \times 40 = 40$.

Step 8: Now, multiply those 4 tens by 7 tens. So, that's 40 x 70 = 2800, or 28 hundreds! Put the 8 under the line in the hundreds column and the 2 up to carry over.

Carry the 2 over up here. Good thing you crossed out the 3!

$7 \times 4 = 28$

The 8 goes in the hundreds column because $40 \times 70 = 2800$.

Step 9: Time to multiply those 4 tens by 2 hundreds. So, 40 x 200 = 8000, but you need add the amount carried over from the last step. That gives you 10 thousands. Write the 0 in your thousands column. You NOW have a 1 to carry over, so write a teeny 1 at the top of the ten thousands column.

$2 \times 4 = 8$

But remember, you have those extra 2 thousands that you carried over from the last step! $2 + 8 = 10$

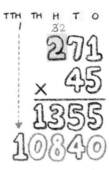

Put the 0 from your ten here.

Step 10: There's nothing left to multiply, but you've got to bring that 1 ten thousand down to the left of the zero. The multiplying part is all done!

Step 11: Now that you've multiplied all of the digits in the number on the top row by all of the digits in the number on the bottom row, add your two answer lines together using **column addition**. You're so close now, but you still have to deal with decimals and then round your answer!

TTH TH H T O

271
× 45
1355
+ 10840
12195

Start with a pretend decimal point here, and move it two spots to the left.

121.95.

2 1

121.95

Step 12: This is the fun part! You started with a number with two decimal places. Time to put them back! Throw a pretend decimal point next to the last digit, then step it to the left two times because you know your final answer will have two decimal places.

Here's the ones spot

Look to the digit on the right.

121.95

Step 13: Now for some rounding! The question asked for an answer that is to the nearest kilogram. So, you've got a 1 in the ones spot. Look to the digit to the right of that one. It's a 9 — and that's definitely more than 5, so you're rounding up. The digits to the right of the ones spot flip to zero, and you add 1 to the ones spot. 121 + 1 = 122.

We added the 1 over here

When you go to write your answer, you don't need to include the zeros.

122.00

A: 271 lbs rounded to the nearest full kilogram is 122 kg.

ROUNDING REFRESHER!
Look to the digit on the right of the place value you are rounding to. If it's 5 or more, round up! If it's 4 or less, round down.

MONEY

Making Dollars Make Sense!

What even is it?! **Money** is a way to measure how much something is worth. We can use it to buy things. We earn, or get, money if we have a job or an allowance. Money is seriously math in action — we use it every day!

How do we measure money? Just like we have rulers for measuring length, we have something called **currency** to measure money! There are different currencies all over the world — money looks different everywhere! In Canada, we use **dollars** and **cents** to talk about money, and our tools are coins and bills!

We use a symbol to represent dollars, which looks like this: $. It goes before the amount, so $1.50. There's a different symbol for cents, which looks like this: ¢. It goes after the amount, so 150¢. But we NEVER use these symbols together! We choose if we're going to be talking about money amounts in dollars OR cents, and then use the symbol that matches that. You can have $1.50 (dollars) OR you can have 150¢ (cents). But you can't have $1.50¢!

There are 100 cents in 1 dollar. So, 1 dollar = 100 cents!

CURRENCY WORTH LESS THAN 1 DOLLAR

NAME	VALUE	CONVERSIONS/MAKING CHANGE WITH FEWEST POSSIBLE COINS OR BILLS:
nickel	5 cents	N/A
dime	10 cents	2 nickels
quarter	25 cents	2 dimes + 1 nickel

There are different ways we can turn 25 cents into other coins. Here we used 2 dimes and 1 nickel to make a quarter because that's only 3 total coins. We also could have used 5 nickels, but that's 5 coins, so we don't want to do that! When we have to carry lots and lots of coins, they can get heavy! That's why we want to use the fewest number of coins possible.

In Real, Actual Life!

In Canada we used to use pennies, which were worth 1 cent each. We don't use physical pennies anymore, but cents still exist in the prices we pay. It's no big deal if we're paying with a debit or credit card. Your account is charged the exact price. But without pennies we have a problem when we're paying with cash! To solve it, we round to the nearest 5 cents. Remember how to round? Sure you do! We use the same rounding rules to round money amounts. So, let's say you buy something with cash that costs $1.53. Are you going to round DOWN to $1.50 or round UP to $1.55? Well, since 3 is closer to 5, we round UP to $1.55, and that's how much you pay. This will be a handy trick to have in your pocket along with your coins.

CURRENCY WORTH 1 DOLLAR OR MORE

NAME	VALUE	CONVERSIONS/MAKING CHANGE WITH FEWEST POSSIBLE COINS OR BILLS:
loonie	100 cents or 1 dollar	4 quarters
toonie	200 cents or 2 dollars	2 loonies
5-dollar bill	500 cents or 5 dollars	2 toonies + 1 loonie
10-dollar bill	1000 cents or 10 dollars	2 5-dollar bills
20-dollar bill	2000 cents or 20 dollars	2 10-dollar bills

MONEY AMOUNTS ARE JUST LIKE DECIMAL NUMBERS!

Cool, right? And the thing is, since there are 100 cents in a dollar, we don't need to have more than two decimal places, because the second decimal place is for hundredths (or pennies), and that's as far as we need to go!

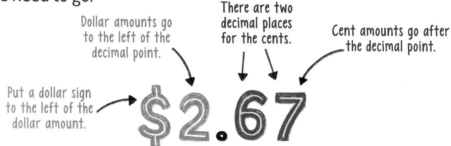

There are two decimal places for the cents.

Dollar amounts go to the left of the decimal point.

Cent amounts go after the decimal point.

Put a dollar sign to the left of the dollar amount.

$2.67

SAY IT OUT LOUD!

We read money amounts the same way we read out decimal places. The decimal point is like the word "and." Instead of naming each digit's place value, we say the word "dollars" after the dollar amount, and the word "cents" after the digits in our decimal places. So, $2.67 would be "two DOLLARS and 67 CENTS!"

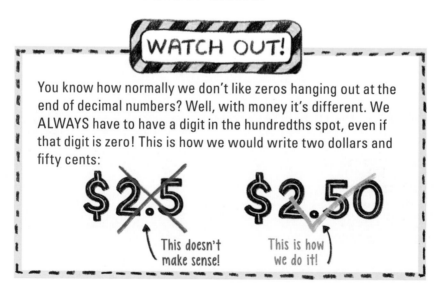

WATCH OUT!

You know how normally we don't like zeros hanging out at the end of decimal numbers? Well, with money it's different. We ALWAYS have to have a digit in the hundredths spot, even if that digit is zero! This is how we would write two dollars and fifty cents:

$2.5
This doesn't make sense!

$2.50
This is how we do it!

160

CONVERTING BETWEEN DOLLARS AND CENTS

Units of currency are like ALL of the other units of measurement we've been learning about: you CAN'T do math with them unless all of your amounts are in the same unit! The good news is that there are only two currency units: dollars and cents! To switch from dollars to cents, we multiply by 100. To switch from cents to dollars, we divide by 100.

From BIG units to SMALL units:

DOLLARS to CENTS

× **100**

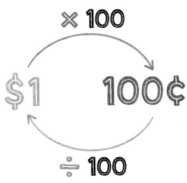

$1   100¢

÷ **100**

CENTS to DOLLARS

From SMALL units to BIG units:

COOL COIN COMBINATIONS!

We can make the SAME cash amount using DIFFERENT coin combinations, which is so cool! Using fewer coins is easier to understand, so here are some examples of how it works.

Q: Find three different coin combinations to make $1.45.

COOL COMBOS! There are LOTS of right answers to this question!

Combo #1

1 loonie	1 quarter	2 dimes
Value: $1.00 or 100¢	Value: $0.25 or 25¢	Value: $0.20 or 20¢

Total value: $1.45   Total number of coins used: 4

Combo #2

1 loonie	4 dimes	1 nickel
Value: $1.00 or 100¢	Value: $0.40 or 40¢	Value: $0.05 or 5¢

Total value: $1.45   Total number of coins used: 6

Combo #3

5 quarters	2 dimes
Value: $1.25 or 125¢	Value: $0.20 or 20¢

Total value: $1.45   Total number of coins used: 7

Doing Actual Math with Money!

We can add, subtract, multiply and divide with money just like we do with other numbers! We can even do it in our heads (if we love mental math!), or we can just use the same methods we use for doing math with decimals because dollars and cents are just decimal numbers with dollar signs in front of them. Cha-ching!

Simple Money Math

Q: You're planning a party for your besties and obviously need to stock up on treats. You go to the store and grab gumballs, chocolate bars and ice cream. Their prices are listed on the shelf. How much are you spending in total on your sugar fest?

Step 1: All you're doing is adding your amounts together, just like you would add normal decimal numbers. BUT you know what you have to do first, right? MAKE SURE ALL MONEY AMOUNTS ARE IN THE SAME UNIT! So, do that first. Switch everything to dollars OR cents – you pick. Because two of the prices are already in dollars, stick with that and just convert the gumball price into dollars too! To do that, you divide it by 100.

$$50 \div 100 = 0.5$$

So, your gumballs cost $0.50

Step 2: Now, add 'em all up! You can use column addition — so simple! You can drop the dollar signs when you're adding, because you really don't need them until the end.

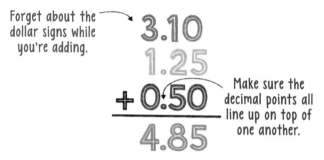

Forget about the dollar signs while you're adding.

$$
\begin{array}{r}
3.10 \\
1.25 \\
+ \ 0.50 \\
\hline
4.85
\end{array}
$$

Make sure the decimal points all line up on top of one another.

Step 3: Stick a dollar sign in front of your number, and you're done! Now your answer looks like this:

$$\$4.85$$

A: The total cost of all of your yummy treats is $4.85.

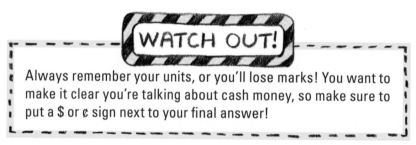

WATCH OUT!

Always remember your units, or you'll lose marks! You want to make it clear you're talking about cash money, so make sure to put a $ or ¢ sign next to your final answer!

PRO MONEY MATH: MAKING CHANGE!

When we pay for things, we give money to a cashier and often get some money back. We call this **making change**! It's good to know exactly how much you should be getting back, just in case they make a mistake, 'cause mistakes happen. But that's simple! All you need to do is find the DIFFERENCE between how much money you passed over and how much the thing you paid for cost. The word "difference" just means SUBTRACTION!

Q: So, remember all those treats you bought? Well, you paid for them with a 5-dollar bill. But, hey . . . that's more money than they cost! How much money should the cashier give you back?

Step 1: Normally with this sort of question, the first step is to find the total amount (so add up) the cost of all of the things you're buying. You already did that in the last question (hurray!), so you can skip this step. You know that all of your treats cost $4.85.

Step 2: Now, you just need to find the difference between $5.00 and $4.85. To do this, use column subtraction and subtract the smaller number from the bigger one. Remember to add a decimal point and two zeros to your $5 so that everything lines up!

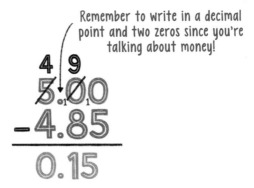

Remember to write in a decimal point and two zeros since you're talking about money!

Step 3: Now, remember to write in your units! You can write your answer as $0.15, or because the amount is less than a dollar, you can write it in cents like this: 15¢.

A: The change you get from paying for your treats with a 5-dollar bill is 15¢.

In Real, Actual Life!

So you may know about **taxes** and that there's such a thing as a sales tax. When you buy something, a percentage of your total gets added onto the total. Then you have a new total — and it's now MORE than the total of just the items. But we still need to pay it — this is how most governments raise money to pay for hospitals and roads and other things we all share in our communities.

Want MORE Math Hacks²?

For more on calculating percentages, what a ratio is, the secret of BEDMAS, extra examples of questions and SO much more, visit: www.scholastic.ca/math-hacks

INDEX